A Word

A word. One word. Well, two. Thank you. Thank you to the people who populate these stories, for being my families and friends. Thank you for living rich lives and thus enriching mine. Thank you to members of Beverly's Sand Box Bunch who listened and encouraged me.

My gratitude to Derek Love who was first to designate these little stories, "a book, Gran." Thank you also to Sarah Love, Katie Love and Jamie Love for the illustrations. My excellent friend Anita McCreery modified Sarah's photograph to create the cover of this edition.

The title, Tell Me a Story, came from a child. When Sarah was about 10, she continued to sit at the kitchen table after her sisters had raced away to play. I asked, "Sarah, is there anything else you want? More milk?"

She patted the table. "Gran, tell me a story. Tell me a story about my daddy when he was my age." I told her one then and have continued.

Particular appreciation goes to son John Love who made this book come true.

It is dedicated to my grandchildren, to theirs, and to yours when you write your stories. Remember, you don't have to start at the beginning!

Donna Rankin Love
Winter 2007

Table of Contents

Beverly's Sandbox...1
Flinty..3
To Have and to Hold 5
Fourth Street 10
I Always Wanted to Be.....................................12
The Back Yard on Coulter Street....................14
Shopping..16
Our Father who art..19
I Remember Ben 28
The Room Behind His Office 32
The Day We Lost Sam.......................................34
Our Very Own Second Grade Drop-out...............37
Deedle Deedle Dumpling, My Son John..............40
It's Been Quite A Day!......................................49
Feet 52
It's in the Bag!..54
Penny Harper and the Giraffe.........................57
March Miracles..59
Gene Gordon and The Great Peace March.........62
The Eighteenth Great Peace March Reunion 65
Pay Back..69
Good Morning! 70
Rush to the Rescue 73
Picking Blackberries.......................................74
What's a Fence?...77
Dawning of a Friendship.................................78
More Watermelon, Please.................................79
One Last Boat in the Bay 81
I Hear You, Mother! 85
Christmastime, Again!.....................................89
I Said No 93
And Here's Jamie!..96
Look in the Drawer..100
Celebrating Jenny..103
I Bought a Car Yesterday!................................109
A Peek at a Part of Alaska 114
Showed Up and Joined Up................................117
What's A Groover?..122
Easter Eve in the Desert.................................125
I Got It Back!..127
Things They've Said 131
Commencement Speeches..................................134

Beverly's Sandbox

As though in a sandbox, the members of Life Long Learner's Writing Group gather around Beverly's dining table. On Fridays in the bright winter of 2005, our parent drops us off at the curb and we grey-haired children troop up the steps, push through the front door, and choose our favorite places.

Ed, a shiny boy who wears ironed shirts and probably has a linen handkerchief in his pocket, chooses a chair with his back to the kitchen. Elizabeth likes her back to the windows, her blue eyes sensitive to light. Beverly, a cute, tidy, polite girl sits at the head of the table. After all, it's her sandbox, and she gives us refreshments in pretty little china cups. Dot on one side of Beverly and Elaine on the other have been friends for a long time. Red haired, chatty Breda seems content to sit anywhere. And Shirley, the new girl in town, sits and smiles at everyone. Dave often sits next to Elaine. I like to sit next to Ed because when I was new and unsure, he was friendly and kind.

Ed, a real engineer, has a big strong castle; he's writing his life into a permanent record for succeeding generations of his family. Elizabeth a poet, a weaver of words, builds with delicate, subtle turns and twists. Listening to her poems has inspired me to take the dusty books of poetry off the top shelves at home to read aloud. Dot's castle is tall and intricate, full of details from her vivid memories. Her humor lifts us while Elaine's recounting of courage in dangerous times is almost belied by her mischievous twinkle that has survived. In every sandbox is a boy who is so bright and has learned so many big words that the rest are confused by his lofty discourse. Dave just can't help being that boy in our group. Shirley listens eagerly to Dave and says, "Oh, I like that, Dave! My husband used to build his castle as you have built yours." I don't have a castle so much as a village cluster of little houses for my grandchildren.

We each have our project, our castle, our creation, our reality infused with imagination. We help each other rearrange the ramparts, decorate with shells and flags, revise, improve the construction and appeal of our works. In this sandbox I never feel that no matter how hard I try, it's not good enough. Here, no matter what we make, it is good. At the least, a good beginning.

Playmates with our lives as our playground, we share, take turns, cooperate, and are considerate. We are the kind who are asked back. We are gentle children, old enough to know to be nice, young enough to be natural, honest and direct. Maybe now we are six.

We are in our sandbox, children with grandparent faces.

Flinty

"Flinty," the article in the December 2004, Smithsonian magazine says about the Rev. John Rankin. A "flinty Tennessean who moved north to escape the atmosphere of slavery." I like that.

In a log cabin at the headwaters of Assumption Creek in the wilderness of East Tennessee, John was born to Jane and Richard Rankin on February 4, 1793. He was the fourth of 11 sons and one daughter and is my Great-great grandfather. His parents wanted a simple life for him but his wasn't to be simple. He was flinty. He became a Presbyterian minister and a friend of the Rev Henry Ward Beecher, who, when asked "Who abolished slavery?" answered, "The Rev John Rankin and his sons did it."

John Rankin began his career when he wrote a series of letters denouncing his brother's recent purchase of a slave in Virginia. These letters were published and influenced others. The Rankins' simple brick farmhouse, which still stands today in Ripley, Ohio, is on a hill top, visible for miles along the Ohio River and well into Kentucky. Here, slaves were fed, hidden for a brief time and led along an overgrown creek-bed or through corn fields to the next "station" a few miles north. Ripley became the front line where abolitionists and slave chasers confronted each other.

The magazine article says, "Since the 1820's, a network of radical white Presbyterians, led by the Rev John Rankin, collaborated with local blacks on both sides of the river in one of the most successful underground operations."

I grew up hearing family stories. As a child, I listened wide eyed and breathless while Grandmother Sarah, our father's mother, widow of John DeLoss Rankin, told about a poor little slave girl named Eliza who escaped by jumping from one ice chunk to the next as she fled across the Ohio River. "And," Grandmother said, "Eliza made it to the other side, still clutching her baby. As she dragged herself up the far riverbank, four big white boys stepped from the bushes and grabbed her. They hurried her up the hill to their father's house, rushed her inside and slammed the door shut." I was always relieved when Grandmother told us, "They sat her down by the fire. Their mother brought her some warm food and dry clothes." That true story was in Uncle Tom's Cabin by Harriet Beecher Stowe, daughter of the Rev. Beecher. The book is said to have inflamed indignant readers and may have even started the Civil War. Those boys from the bushes were four of Jean and John Rankin's nine sons.

A story I especially like is about another one of John Rankin's sons, Thomas Lovejoy, who in the early 1860's escorted four runaway slaves from Ripley all the way to Chatham, Canada. Thomas sat up with the black driver of the carriage while the slaves sat inside. The driver told his own story of escape from Kentucky in which a gentleman and his sons helped. "Well," he concluded, "I'd just like to have that gentleman know that I am one of the colored men that prospered in Canada, and I owe it all to him that I ever got here." As they arrived at their destination, Thomas paid the driver the $1.50 fare and said, "I can tell him."

"Are you sure?" the driver asked.

"Yes, I surely will. That man is my father."

The driver broke down. "Take back that money, take that money! It burns my hands!"*

❦

In August 2004, in Cincinnati, a new museum, The National Underground Railroad Freedom Center, opened. It is the first permanent museum exhibit to chronicle the stories of slaves, slave owners, slave hunters, and abolitionists. John Rankin is featured. I want to go to Cincinnati and to Ripley. I want my families to go. I like to think a drop of that flinty blood still flows in our veins.

❦

Webster's New Collegiate Dictionary, 1974: "Flint: a massive hard quartz that produces a spark when struck by steel. Flinty: unyielding."

* Beyond the River, by Ann Hagedorn, page 271.

Tell Me a Story

To Have and To Hold

The summer days of 1926 were passing. On Monday, August 2, Mildred Taylor, in her parents' home out in the Westmorland neighborhood of Portland, Oregon, got up, dressed, looked in the mirror and said, "I've had enough of what they want. I'm going to do something about what we want." She was 24. Smart. Popular. Pretty bobbed auburn hair with a wave above her left eye. She had attended stenography school in Portland, and enjoyed a good job. She lived at home and paid rent to her mother and dad as well as contributing to her brother Ralph's tuition to University of Oregon Medical School. Each day Mildred took the bus downtown to the law offices where she was secretary to Joe Carson. On the weekends, she wore the practical jacket her mother had made for her and hiked the mountains and beaches with friends.

That group included Jack Rankin, a student at the University of Oregon Medical School. The med school had had the best parties in Portland with alcohol directly from the school labs mixed with grapefruit juice. Mildred had gone with her brother Ralph and had met Jack about a year ago. They were in love and had talked of marriage.

Jack had asked Mildred to marry him in September after he'd finished his summer job. They could move together to Pendleton, in eastern Oregon, where he'd serve his internship. Their housing would be free and he would have a little money. He was certain they could get by. "It'll be an adventure," he'd said.

When she heard about their plans, Mildred's mother was determined that they would have a big wedding in which Vera, her other daughter, would play the piano. "And" her mother had decided, "Aunt Lue can sing. And your cousin Pearl Owings can play her violin." Mildred had winced.

When Jack told his mother, she whined that she didn't want him to marry at all. "You can live with me." she had whimpered. "I'll take care of you as only a mother can." She blew her nose. Mildred clenched her teeth and said nothing when Jack reported this.

On the bus that morning, she rehearsed what she would say to her boss. She didn't want to jeopardize her job. She liked her salary of $100.00 a month. She shuddered at the thought of her mother's fury. Lena Taylor was a short, stout volatile powerhouse of a woman who could explode and break dishes. Her father would continue to be his quiet, agreeable self, no matter what. She didn't give a hoot about Jack's mother. "Nothing but a sniveler," she muttered. Vera would understand if she didn't ask her to play the piano. After all, Vera had dealt with their Mother's controlling ways by eloping.

Downtown, Mildred lay her purse and hat on her desk and walked directly to Joe Carson's office door. She knocked. He bellowed, "Come in!"

She smiled at her boss, a bear of a man. He was pleasantly plump, shorter than average; an admirable, authoritative, brusque person with a quick temper. Mildred recalled the times they "ruffled each other." Once she had been so angry at him, she had gone to the Employment Bureau to look for another job. The Employment Bureau lady must have called the office to check on her. When Mildred returned about noon, Joe called her in and said, "Taylor, you and I both have quick tempers. When you get angry with me or I get angry with you, you keep cool. If we both get angry at the same time, God, how the feathers will fly."

She hoped he wouldn't be angry this morning. "Come in, Taylor." He looked up from the papers on his heavy dark oak desk. "What do you want?"

"Well," she said, "I'd like to have the day off."

"Today? Today is Monday. You know Mondays are always busy. Why the hell would you want to take off today?"

She stood still, forced her hands to relax at her sides, clutched only with her right thumb and forefinger at a pleat in her skirt. "I'd like to be married this afternoon."

"Married! Well, hell, yes! Take off the whole day and God bless you!".

She went to her desk to phone Jack who was visiting his mother out on 82nd St. for a long weekend from his summer job at a small hospital in Redmond, WA.

When Jack answered her phone call, Mildred explained, "I want us to be married this afternoon in a simple at-home wedding like we've always wanted. I know we'd planned to be married in September, but I'm tired of my mother trying to make it into something big and lavish. Dad can't afford the wedding she wants us to have." She rushed on. "Just because Vera ran off to the court house with Dick Onthank and then telephoned Mother to announce her wedding doesn't mean I have to make up for it." A stop for breath. "Meet me downtown at the entrance of the Henry Building in an hour."

"Well, ok. I'll meet you." He sounded stunned. "I'm standing here in my sock feet and my mother is right here in the kitchen, too. I'll ask to borrow her car. No, I won't get into it with her. What about your mother? I thought she wanted your sister Vera to sing. We can talk more about it when I get there."

She picked up the phone again, took a big breath and said, "Mother, Jack and I want to be married today."

She heard only a silence and then, "Today! Today! Why today? Are you sure?"

Mildred's stomach churned with anxiety. "Yes, Mother, I am sure. Jack is coming downtown to pick me up and we'll be married at home just as I've promised you. A simple ceremony, though."

Her mother started to raise her voice, "You know what I've wanted for you!" And Mildred interrupted, "Yes, Mother, and I know you are disappointed but I'm making the arrangements for two o'clock this afternoon. Will you call Dad and ask him to come home early?"

Her mother huffed and grunted, "Oh, all right," Mildred could imagine her mother slamming the receiver onto its hook.

Then, Jack's mother. She sat down, took another breath, gave the number to the operator, and said, "I'm calling to tell you that Jack and I will be married this afternoon. Yes, well, in spite of that, we have decided. I'm sorry you feel that way. Would you like to bring your minister? And his wife too, if you wish. Thank you. We will meet at two o'clock at my parents' home. Yes, 19th Street."

Jack arrived downtown in his mother's old Ford touring car. He grinned as he pulled up to the curb. "Well! Bobby!" he exclaimed, using a pet nick-name for her, "when you decide, you make things happen, don't you!" She returned his excited hug. They drove to the Multnomah County Court House to get the wedding license, parked the car, and ran up the stairs. He took them two at a time pulling Mildred along, both laughing.

The license accomplished, she asked Jack to stop by a jewelry store to buy the ring. "Wait," he said, "I don't have enough money for a ring. Do we have to have a ring? Maybe we can borrow one. Temporarily, of course. Or we could postpone the whole thing." She didn't notice the cloud of humiliation across his face.

"No, and not a borrowed ring." she was adamant. "I'll buy it." Mildred jumped out of the car, swung into the store and bought her own plain gold wedding band. Jack saw a corner flower stand and bought a bouquet of summer flowers. When his bride came out of the store, he handed them to her. "One day I'll make it up to you." he promised.

They went on out to her parents' home. Jack strode into the kitchen where Mildred's mother was finishing up the lunch dishes. "I'm too busy to talk to you now, Jack, and my husband is in our bedroom changing his shirt." Jack stood, filling the doorway with his 6' 2" frame, and jammed his hands into his pockets.

Upstairs, Mildred freshened her rouge, brushed her hair and put on the dress she had worn when they had first met and begun dating. He liked the cranberry brocade. "It suits you," he had said. She felt feminine. Like a bride.

At two o'clock seven people, the bride's parents, the groom's mother, the minister and his wife, and the wedding couple gathered in front of the fireplace in the living room. The minister's wife, the mother-of-the-groom and the father-of-the-bride stood. The mother-of-the-bride kept her apron on and sat over to one side. In a few minutes Jack and Mildred were married.

The couple quickly kissed, squeezed hands, and turned toward their parents. John Taylor shyly hugged his youngest child and shook Jack's hand. Lena Taylor folded her arms. Mildred noticed that the front of Jack's mother's blue satin dress was splattered with tearstains. After a few formalities, Mildred rode with Jack down to the Southern Pacific train station where they sat on a bench and

made plans for their life together. He went back to Redmond on the five o'clock. Mildred dutifully returned his mother's car and took the streetcar to her parents' home, where she went up to her room and put her bridal bouquet in water. She rocked back and forth in a small rocker, stared out the window and held her future in front of her.

She was back in the office by 8:30 Tuesday morning. Joe Carson came out of his office, "Well, good morning and welcome, Mrs. Rankin."

The following weekend they found a small apartment out in the St. John's area. After Jack's summer job was completed, the newlyweds spent a honeymoon week at Cannon Beach in his brother Jerry's tiny beach cabin. In September they moved to Pendleton.

They had 59 married years together before Jack died in November 1985, at the age of 88. Mother helped me with the details of this story when she was 100, a few months before she died in November of 2002.

Fourth Street

Our family still lived on West Fourth Street in Coquille, so I must have been no more than seven, John five, and Richard just a bright-eyed baby. Probably 1934. The Craftsman style house at the end of Fourth Street stood two-stories, warm and wooden with a side yard for playing ball if we didn't trample Mother's crescent shaped flower bed of yellow and orange marigolds. The myrtlewood tree was a strong green giant supporting our tree house. Swings dangled from its branches. Knobbly old twists of apple trees congregated at the corner of the house.

Across the back edge of the yard random fence boards, banded together by brambles and roses, leaned carelessly behind gladiolas and Sweet William. In the rear corner hunched the gabled garage and from it the driveway stretched out straight to the street. On this level strip of concrete, John pedaled his red racing tricycle and I learned to skate. Behind the garage, beyond the berry vines on the fence, lay an unpaved alley.

From the alley, the hobos appeared at the back gate. They came, never more than one at a time, ducking beneath the clothes lines, shuffling to the base of the back porch steps. They stood there, rough, brown, shapeless, sometimes reaching forward to tap once or twice, and waited for Mother to peer through the screen door.

"Need some wood chopped, Ma'm? I can weed and hoe. Paint? Sweep that long driveway? Those apple trees could stand some trimmin'."

They never asked for charity. They asked for work and a meal. I remember the whack of the axe splitting wood. To eat, they sat down on the lowest of the back steps or on the chopping block next to the axe. They didn't talk much, but John and I thought they were wonderful men with lives of adventure. They patted us on the heads and smiled down on us when we were allowed to give them an apple. Sometimes we sat on the steps with one of them and ate, too.

When the hobo was through wiping the last bit of food with the last bite of bread, he'd stand up, hand Mother his plate, thank her, and touch the brim of his hat. He'd drift away, out the back gate, and down the alley between the tin trashcans and bristling briars. Each one shouldered a rusty canvas knapsack or a lumpy gunnysack. They all walked. Slowly, quietly, easily. Never in a hurry. Some turned at the end of the alley to wave before disappearing around the corner.

A favorite of Mother's named Roy was out by the garage chopping wood late one afternoon while John and I knelt on the worn floor of the back porch playing cars. "Udden udden" was all I could sound. John, being a boy, could make wonderful mechanical gear-shifting, logging-truck roars. We sensed more than saw that Roy had stopped, straightened, and turned to squint down the driveway. Shaded by his cocked arm, his eyes widened. He grinned a little and nodded twice. "Yes, SIR!" he said.

"What does he see?" John leaned out over the porch railing.

Mother called to us even before she slipped through the kitchen door. "Daddy's home! Come along, let's go see him!"

"Why is she so excited?" I asked. We abandoned our brightly painted lead cars to follow her down the walk. That wasn't Daddy. At least that wasn't his car. His car was drab grey and full of country-doctor dust. Maybe it was Uncle Glenn? No, his car was fire-chief red and he always sent us a trill with the siren from about a block away. The windshield mirrored only trees and sky.

The car easing toward us was a pale silvery blue. Light quivered and shimmered and reflected on the chrome of the bumper, of the window frames, off the headlight rims, and from the edge of the running board. The entire car vibrated with light. The sun setting beyond Fourth Street formed a halo. It was the most extravagantly beautiful car I had ever seen. Rounded lines, gentle curves, a sleek slope of a trunk, more surfaces that turned, swept, arched, bowed, curled and crested.

John and I walked all around it, then stood quietly together, thoroughly dazzled. Mother wiped her hand on her apron before she reached over to stroke the hood ornament. On the driver's side, the window lowered. Daddy leaned out. His grin was as bright as the car.

"Move that tricycle. Open the garage. I bought us a Lincoln Zephyr."

I Always Wanted to Be

Until the Community Building in Coquille was constructed in 1940, the three large gathering spaces in town were the high school gym, St. James Episcopal Church Guild Hall, and the IOOF (International Order of Odd Fellows) Lodge Hall upstairs above Lorenz's Clothing Store.

Twelve of us grade-school girls lined ourselves in a row in the meeting room of the IOOF Hall. "Position One!" shouted the ballet teacher as she planted her heels together, toes pointing toward opposite walls. She lifted her arms parallel to the floor and cocked her wrists. Her back lengthened, her neck arched. We girls were in the fifth grade and still pudgy. I wondered how such an elegant creature as Miss Danielson had found her way in 1937 to our small town of Coquille in Southwestern Oregon. To me she was a Fairy Godmother come to grant our wishes. Even better than the barber's wife who had taught us how to draw holly leaves and berries on recipe cards as Christmas gifts.

We sticky little girls stretched and teetered as we learned each position. We accomplished leaping tour jetés diagonally across the room. We thundered and pirouetted about. We never were graduated to toe shoes, but in two years we wore out and outgrew several pairs of classic black ballet slippers.

There were, of course, recitals. The first year, Doris Ann Woods and I were butterflies. We were dressed in our mothers' black Jantzen bathing suits and had attached to our backs huge wings made from coat hanger wire and colorful, geometric patterns of cellophane. On our heads were black hairnets with ties beneath our chins and pipe-cleaner antenna bobbing above our foreheads. I used to have a photo of the two of us. Doris Ann about five inches shorter than I, with a cute little girl body with dimpled knees and dimpled smile. She has lengthened her back and gracefully arched her neck. I am standing in Position Two with locked knees, head tilted to one side in an effort to look shorter, and my arms parallel to the floor as they held open the cellophane butterfly wings.

In the dance, Doris Ann and I flitted about and worked our wings. From one huge flower blossom to another we danced until the entire stage of St. James Episcopal Church Guild Hall was filled with a garden of activated, twirling, swaying, heavily breathing, glistening girl flowers. Miss Danielson glowed as she joined us for curtain calls.

The next year, on the same stage in the Guild Hall, we were in sixth grade. Doris Ann wasn't any taller, but I was. In the row of girls clad in fluffy, yellow organza dresses and ruffled ankle-length pantaloons, Doris Ann was placed at the short girls' end and I was at the opposite. We trailed around after each other among lattice screens festooned with pastel crepe paper roses.

In the finale, we were lined across stage front. Arms extended, backs straight, heads held high, we each slid our right leg along the floor directly in front, paused with toes pointed. In unison, the right legs drew around and extended behind as we bent our left knees and with consummate grace, folded our bodies in a deep bow, heads almost to the floor, arms still parallel to the floor. It was perfect. Almost. My extended right leg stretched clear to the base of one of the trellises and it came crashing forward over us all.

Even though Mother said it wasn't mine but Gwen Elrod's foot at fault, that was the end of my ballet career. Miss Danielson moved away. When I was nineteen, I saw the Rockettes in New York, watched the dancer at the tall end of the line and pretended. When I view "Swan Lake," I can feel myself taking tiny choreographed steps.

Just last week I was sighing, "In my next life, I'll be a dancer."

The Back Yard on Coulter Street

"Swing me higher! Push so I can kick the top of the hedge!" My shiny, blue-eyed brother John was pushing me in the swing in the back yard on Coulter Street. The ropes hung from a tall wooden frame erected just for the swings. We soared. My skirt swept the dust on the way up and clung to my legs on the way down. I loved the feeling of touching the sky and returning safely.

It's been a long time since my brothers and I played in the yard behind the house on Coulter Street in Coquille. We moved there from Fourth Street in the summer before I was in Third Grade. The back yard was about 50 feet from the wooden back porch across the concrete "flagstones", beyond the tall, white trellis, to the back wall lined with foxgloves and bleeding hearts. From the broad white slats of the side fence to the laurel hedge between the next-door neighbors and us, the grass spanned 100 feet. A Northern Spy apple tree grew near the swings. In it, the tree house, and beneath it, our play house which in turn was a fort, puppet theater, tea party house. John, twenty months younger than I, sometimes whispered, "Come on, let's hide in the fort from Richard." Richard, four years younger than John, was still a preschooler.

During sunny childhood summers, John and I hung blankets on the clotheslines to make booths. We held sideshows. Crayoned signs tacked on the front fence advertised, "Pay a Penny. See a Swimming Match". Richard would race eagerly into the house to get a penny from Mother. "Gotch a pinny," he'd announce breathlessly and drop it into our celluloid cash box. We allowed him to peek through the crack between the blankets. He saw a wooden match swimming in a saucer of water. He was young but knew when he'd been had. His dark eyes teared with disappointment as he ran yowling back into the house.

Then we'd have to let him watch our puppet show for free. He paid for lemonade. With the neighborhood kids, he'd line up, pay a penny, get a cup of lemonade made with real lemons and white sugar, and sit on the grass beneath the apple tree. John and I wiggled our hand puppets in a drama full of conflict, shouting, and sudden resolution.

When I was entering the teen years and dazed by the poignant romance of life, I sat on the garden bench sheltered by the white trellis. It was covered with red, red roses. Curled there with House of Seven Gables, I'd read and dream of far-away places. In late spring, the fragrance of daphne wafted me far from Coquille. In summer, flowers blossomed brightly beneath Mother and Pop's bedroom windows. By then, sturdy, red-haired David, the youngest brother, was three.

I got a camera for my thirteenth birthday. "Want your picture taken?" I asked. "John! Richard! David! Line up in front of the flowers!" I aimed the Brownie at them. Then Richard stepped forward and stretched his t-shirt with a picture of Golden Gate Bridge across his round tummy and I moved in close to take a photo of only the bridge. We waited anxious days to get the snapshots back from Bill Barrow's Drug Store. The lineup of three healthy, summertime boys was appealing. The experiment didn't work. The bridge looked warped and I got his hands.

Mother had had an Easy Ringer Washing Machine in the basement, with the clotheslines in the side yard, near the basement steps. When a new Bendix Automatic Washer, the first one in Coquille, was installed along a kitchen wall, the lines were moved nearer the back door, behind the trellis. One whippy spring day when I was sixteen, I was hanging out the clothes. Pop sauntered out, his tall frame relaxed and easy. He stood a bit, watching me, then announced, "Your mother and I have decided that next year you will go to boarding school at St. Helen's Hall in Portland."

Portland! A far-away place. Over the hedge. Up to the sky. Out of the back yard.

Shopping

"Hurry!" my mother called impatiently up the stairs. "We have lots to do today." I was eighteen years old and it was August. Mother was taking me shopping for The Fall Wardrobe.

I hurried down to go out the door with her to the car. Our town in southwestern Oregon was small, but 20 miles away was Coos Bay with a population of 7,000 and two good clothing stores.

At the department store, called The Hub, Mother, her face determined, led the way first to the undergarment counters. She ordered six of some things and a dozen of others, two of these and two of those. All white. Nothing as erotic as a red slip nor as evocative as lace.

Then to the shoe department. As a child I had had to wear well-constructed, brown Girl Scout oxfords. They were ugly. Now, at age eighteen and a sophomore at the University of Oregon, I was allowed Spalding saddle shoes. For dressy occasions, black suede sling pumps.

"Oh," Mother said, "we'll need some stockings. Six pairs. Skin tone."

We put the packages into the car and walked up around the corner to Mr. Gittleson's. Harry Gittleson was originally from San Francisco. He'd had a fashion store there before moving north.

Mr. Gittleson liked me and my tall, young shape. When I was trying on clothes in his shop, I felt promising, not hopelessly gangly. I felt as though some day I might learn to enter a room like Katherine Hepburn. I forgot that Mother had told me I should always wear sleeves to cover my arms that were too long, that I should always take care to hide my bony knees, that little could be done about my long jaw. I stood in the dressing room with Mrs. Gittleson, who liked to be called Mrs. Harry, as she asked me about school and what I liked best. Mother sat in one of the comfortable mauve chairs in the salon and enjoyed cups of tea.

Mr. Gittleson brought out suits, slacks, skirts, coats, sweaters, and shirts to show Mother. Those that passed initial inspection were slipped discretely past the edge of the dressing room curtain. Mrs. Harry nodded her approval as she zipped up the skirt of a grey houndstooth suit and handed me a melon cashmere. She removed her own rope of pearls to place ceremoniously down over my bowed head. The jacket was nearly perfect. "Just need to let the sleeves out a bit, dear," she smiled at me.

Yes, the suit was fine. The grey wool slacks passed. The cardigans, the melon cashmere, the pleated Stewart plaid skirt, the black raincoat with the zip-out lining. And, finally, there was the party dress.

Even Mother's eyes brightened. Mr. Gittleson assured us he had had me in mind when ordering this one. It was green taffeta covered over with black lace. The entire dress was black lace over the gleam of green taffeta. The extravagant black sash tied in a big glistening bow at the back. It had self-covered buttons down the front and a full skirt. The hem was below my knees. It was almost sleeveless! I swirled and rustled about. Mr. Gittleson clasped his hands. Mrs. Harry cocked her head and sighed. Mother motioned me to her to examine the lace and, surreptitiously, the price tag.

"I know it's costly, Mrs. Rankin, but it's perfect for Donna." Mr. Gittleson said.

"We'll take it on approval," Mother hedged, "and see what her father says."

That evening after dinner, I put on a pair of new skin-tone stockings, the new black suede sling pumps and the dress. I stood before my father. He looked up from his medical journal, motioned me to turn around, and asked, "How much?"

I tried a Katherine Hepburn stride toward the kitchen and Mother came, wiping her hands on her apron, to stand next to me.

"I know it's expensive," she said, "but it's perfect for her. It's good quality. Well made. It'll last a long time. $78.00"

Did we hold our breath? My father smiled and nodded. "You're growing up to be a nice looking girl." He turned the page and returned to his reading. Mother returned to the kitchen and I floated up to my room, closed the door, and put on a Harry James record to dance.

In September 1987, forty-two years later, my 86-year-old mother came to California to visit. It was her first trip away from Oregon since my father had died two years ago. One morning I came out from my closet carrying a plastic garment bag on a hanger. I hung it on the doorframe, unzipped it, and took out a party dress.

She looked a long moment. "Oh," she smiled mistily, "you still have it."

Our Father who art....

John and I stood beneath the marquee of the Paramount Theater on upper Broadway in Portland. Two small-town kids, brother, 15, and sister, 17, sheltered from the drizzle on a Sunday afternoon in October 1944. We stood in line, waiting for our turn at the box office. Then the usher in a red and black uniform would click on the flashlight and show us the way down the aisle to our seats. Watching a movie in an elegant theater in the biggest town in Oregon was a far cry from the Liberty in Coquille.

John was enrolled for his second (and last) year at Hill Military School and I was a first-year senior at St. Helen's Hall Episcopal School for Girls, two boarding schools where our parents had sent us. We didn't ever talk about it, but we each knew we'd been sent. Not allowed, sent. John and our father tangled and my rebellious, adolescent attitude angered Mother. "You kids'd drive a woman to drink!" she'd declare. For one school year, John and I were in Portland, leaving the younger brothers, Richard and David, home with our parents.

As I recall, we were quiet as we watched the street activity that day on upper Broadway. We felt alone and dependent on each other. A rangy, middle-aged man sauntered by as he casually checked the line. Suddenly he stopped near us, came closer, put his hand on John's shoulder and bellowed, "Hey, aren't you Doc Rankin's kids! You look just like him!" He said he was from Coquille. As he grinned at us, Coquille didn't seem so far away, after all. "I'll tell Doc Rankin I saw you on the streets in Portland. Ha ha!" He gave us each a pat and disappeared down the block.

John and I, astonished, stared at each other. "We're famous!" he giggled. "Well, Pop's famous and we look like him," I countered. "How can that be? You and I don't look anything alike! You are fair-skinned like Mother and I'm brown like Pop. That's right, isn't it?" "I dunno," he said, "come on, the line's moving." I think John wanted to look like Pop. Sometimes he imitated his postures and expressions.

I felt elated. I was proud to be recognized. I was proud of Pop. That man from Coquille surely admired our father. Maybe as much as I admired him. I thought him the final, dependable authority on everything. I believed that he, in a quiet way, understood my restless longing for independence. He didn't use many words with me. His father-daughter discussion about smoking, drinking and necking consisted of one word, "Don't!" Sometimes he invited me to ride along when he made a house call out in the country or back up in the woods. Then he talked about his mother, about his brothers, about his sister who had died in her twenties, and about himself. I'd wait in the car while he checked a pregnant woman or had coffee with a bed-bound patient.

I was pleased that he chose me to go with him. I believed he had a confidence in me that I didn't get from Mother. I could trust him. I was certain of his caring for me, sensed his fatherly confusion and concern. He liked to be with me.

But he didn't have much time for his family. He was busy with his medical practice and he was active in the Lions Club and the Masons; was mayor of Coquille, and sat on the board of the state AMA. When we were children, even as he carved the Christmas turkey, he'd answer the telephone, shrug into his suit jacket, put on his felt hat, take up his bag and disappear out the front door. Mother sighed and carved the turkey until my brothers grew up enough to take over. Our youngest brother David was probably 40, married and himself a father, when Mother exclaimed, "Look at how well David carves the turkey! Isn't that a symphony of accuracy and style!" David blushed and kept on carving.

~❧~

In a way, I'm surprised Pop even knew how to be a father. His own father had died in Glastonbury, Connecticut, when Pop was a boy. The story goes that in 1906 when he was nine and his brother Jerry was twelve, their widowed mother, our Grandmother Sarah, pinned name tags on them, gave them a box of fried chicken and put them on the train to Oregon. "Now, Jack, you stay right with Jerry.

You two don't get separated." George Dallas, the widower Grandmother planned to marry, met the boys in Oregon City and took them to his family farm out toward Gladstone. Grandmother Sarah with her youngest son Charles and daughter Anita came west as soon as the house in Connecticut sold.

After a few years, George Dallas announced that Jerry and Jack would no longer be going to school, that they were to start working the farm full time. When they resisted, he said, "If you live in my house, you do as I say." The two boys left George Dallas and their mother and homesteaded a small property on the Clackamas River. They bought a tent, moved in, and helped each other through high school. Pop told us he became a pearl diver! Then he'd laugh and say, "That's what we called someone who washed dishes in a restaurant."

Both worked. Together, they harvested summer wheat in Eastern Washington. Jerry worked for neighbors as a handyman. One summer Pop worked in a coal mine. At the end of a long day he ran and jumped onto a coal car to ride up. He dragged his right foot a second too long, and left four toes in a row on the inside of the track. When we were little and ran into our parents' bedroom on Sunday mornings, Pop stuck his foot out from under the covers and wiggled his remaining big toe at us. We squealed and jumped back, then piled on him to wrestle.

He told us stories of his young years. He and Jerry fought in World War I. Jerry in the Army in Europe and Pop in the Navy in Honolulu, guarding the back door of America. Off duty, he was on the basketball court and in swimming competitions. He said he always won the swimming races. After the war, he found a rooming house in Eugene and majored in pre-med at University of Oregon. He took 21 hours a semester while working as a lab assistant so he could finish as quickly as possible. "I had to hurry because I didn't have enough money to keep paying tuition." In two years, he was ready for U of O Medical School in Portland.

It was not all work. During Prohibition, the medical school students, with access to laboratory alcohol, gave enviable parties. Girls from downtown attorneys' offices where Mother worked were invited. That's how they met. The two of them, Jack Rankin and

Mildred Taylor, along with other medical school couples, spent Saturdays hiking on Mt Hood and up the Columbia River Gorge. In 1926 he was graduated and that summer got a residency in a small central-Washington hospital. He visited Mother in Portland when he could.

One Monday morning, when Jack had stayed over with his mother out in Gladstone, Mildred called him to say, "I think this is a good day to be married." They were. John De Loss Rankin and Mildred Jean Taylor married at her parents' home in Portland in the afternoon of August 2, 1926. Next day both Jack and Mildred returned to their jobs. At the end of the summer, they moved to Pendleton. He finished his internship at the Oregon State Mental Institution there in 1927. September of that year I was born. Some of my first baby-sitters were benign patients of the Mental Hospital. Mother said one of them turned all the pictures to the face the wall.

We moved to Bandon, in Coos County, where Pop joined a medical office and John was born in 1929. After a few years the family moved to Marshfield (later named Coos Bay) where Richard was born, and finally to Coquille, David's birthplace. Mother has told me that those first ten years were the best. "Very much in love," they were excited about their bright future. Theirs was a large family for the Depression Years. So when Grandmother Sarah or Uncle Jerry needed money and Pop sent it to them, Mother clamped her mouth shut in a hard line.

It bothered her that our family didn't have very much money. Some patients just couldn't pay their bills. Pop accepted what they brought: boxes of produce, a truckload of potatoes for the birth of a baby, oil paintings for gall bladder surgery, a live goat to us children for a stitched-up hand. We had potatoes in every form for an entire winter. Mother hung the seascape over the mantle and the landscape over the buffet in the dining room. We named the goat Billy and played "King of the Mountain" with him.

Our father told us, "I have been president of every organization I ever joined." A hard act to follow. Although proud to be his children, my brothers and I were intimidated by him and listened. He emphasized that education is something no one can take away and recounted his beginnings and achievements. He said we could do anything we set out to do. Still, the unspoken message was, "Be good, be great, but not greater than I, your father."

As a young teenager, I became sullen around my parents and wanted to be out and away. One windy afternoon in my junior year at Coquille High School, I was in the back yard, hanging laundry on the line when Pop came out. He stood a while and watched me, then said, "Your Mother and I have decided you will go to St. Helen's Hall in Portland next year."

Finally! A year later than I'd wanted, but, still, I was to be a boarder. Away! I was so ready! That school year, 1944-45, Pop came to visit whenever he attended a state medical meeting. He took me, just me, not John, to dinner at La Abbey, a French restaurant in the Heathman Hotel. We shared a tureen of Bouillabaisse as he told me of life at home in Coquille.

In mid-January, during one of those dinners, I told him about our English teacher and how I got her fired. I felt clever and wanted him to be pleased with me. He listened as I told him the teacher had not been able to diagram sentences. I had marched, blue pleated skirt swishing, into the assistant principal's office and said, "My parents are paying good money for me to be here and Miss Atcheson can't even diagram a sentence! If she can't do that, I can't understand the structure." After Christmas holiday, the vice-principal took over the class and she could diagram sentences. As I concluded, Pop passed the bread and reminded me to be polite. I wonder if he went home and told Mother. Did he grin? Did she just shrug?

In the Fall of 1945, almost a year since John and I had stood in line at the Paramount Theater, Pop drove me and my trunk the 150 miles from Coquille to the University of Oregon in Eugene. At his suggestion, "can't hurt, might help", I majored in pre-med. I wasn't the student he had been and eventually changed to English and then Psychology. At Thanksgiving my sophomore year I brought home the A paper I'd written about Sinclair Lewis' "Babbitt". Mother, my brothers, Grandmother Taylor and Mother's brother, our Uncle Glenn, gathered around the table and listened to me. I wanted to hear Pop say, "You done good, Sis." He didn't. Instead, he launched into a long tale about his having met Sinclair Lewis and about how he, Pop himself, had partially paid medical school expenses by writing pulp-magazine cowboy stories. Deflated, I promised myself to never, ever bring my accomplishments to him again. I think now he was just adding what he could to the discussion, but at the time I felt upstaged.

As I studied the psychology of family dynamics, I felt I could take a position on father-son relationships. During a University vacation, Pop asked me to once again ride with him to visit a patient down the river near Bandon. While he drove, I told him I thought he'd regret not having spent more time with my brothers. They needed his attention. He didn't make any commitments, but in one of Mother's letters she told me Pop had invited John to go out deep-sea fishing with him. John went, got seasick, and didn't go again, but both Richard and David went whenever they were invited on weekends. They grew to love fishing as much as our father did. In their adult lives, both Richard and David have fishing boats.

Fishing was one of Pop's all-time greatest enthusiasms. He could get away from the telephone and be outdoors. He and Levi Bunch built a 32-foot, plywood, in-board, William Atkin design boat in Levi's barn. The boat, named "The Donna," was seaworthy, had a cabin topped by a windshield, and looked homemade. He loved that boat. On Thursdays, Pop escaped with Levi to the sea. Occasionally Uncle Glenn and once even Uncle Jerry came to go out over the bar at Bandon. They came home with more fish than they could eat. Often Pop delivered fish to the kitchen of his Coquille Hospital, to the Lion's Club barbecue, to the County Poor Farm out Fairview Road, and to all the friends who would receive them. Eventually he took out a commercial fishing license so he could peddle tuna, salmon, and halibut to Mr. Stevens' Market.

Pop found an additional use for his boat. And additional glory for himself. While I was growing up, the entire town celebrated Fourth of July. Signs over the highways in southwestern Oregon proclaimed, "All Roads Lead to Coquille." There were games, log-rolling and pole-climbing contests, dances in the Community Building, music, and food booths. Our usually severe algebra teacher, Mrs. Byers, donned an apron and stood in a booth to call out, "Scones, get your hot scones and jam!" For a while I thought she was selling

stones and wondered why Pop said they were delicious. We had parades. One downtown and one on the Coquille River. "The Donna" was the queen's and her court's float in the river parade. For about a mile from the Smith Wood Products Mill down to the bridge, Pop proudly led the parade with five high school girls in their prom dresses, who sat on the cabin, smiling and waving. Pop smiled and waved, too.

And in all this time of medical prominence and civic achievement, he told me all he really wanted to be was a farmer. He did buy a small farm nine miles downriver, just past Riverton. We lived there the summer I finished eighth grade. John must have been 12, Richard eight, and David four. We had a garden and corn patch, apple trees, one cow named Bessy, a horse named Ribbons, a flock of sheep, lots of chickens and kittens; Bootsie, the Australian shepherd, and Billy, the goat. That summer it seemed everyone was happy....at least most of the time. I was embarrassed about my developing body and Mother was disgusted with my asking for a bra. I heard her at breakfast scoffing to Pop about my request and his reply, "She just looks like two fried eggs on the wall." Perhaps that's the summer my shoulders curved over. I wore big shirts and played with my brothers.

By the time Pop bought a much larger ranch only five miles out Fat Elk Road from town, I was at the University. He loved living out there. Even in winter when the roads were under water. On those days, he'd untie his motorboat from a fence post, and putt across the flooded bottomland, tie up at the creamery, and walk the few blocks to his office in the hospital. During the summer, he rented bottomland pasture to a Texas cattleman as well as hillside acreage to Pic-Sweet Peas, a new business venture in growing and freezing fresh peas. When Jim Love and I were married, August 16, 1949, Pop had the County pave five miles of road out to his ranch. Nothing too good for his daughter.

After a while, Mother didn't like the inconvenience of living outside of town, so they bought an old Georgian house up Second Street in Coquille, remodeled it, and moved in. That was where they lived when Pop found Matt for Jim and me to adopt in 1953. They still lived there when I began driving Jim's and my four sons, Matt, and his brothers, Sam, John, and Marty to Oregon each August. We went primarily to "go to the Lake."

Pop and Mother had found an old yellow farmhouse on Carlson Arm of North Ten-Mile Lake about an hour up Highway 101 from Coquille. Each August my brothers and their families, the Love Boys and I gathered on the public dock in Lakeside so Pop could ferry us to the house. Twenty-four of us, 14 of whom were their grandchildren! One time, as many of us lay around the living room watching old home movies, Pop came stepping carefully among us, his over-night bag in hand. "Where are you going, Pop?" my brother Richard asked. "I'm goin' home. Too damn many people here. I'm takin' the boat. I'll see you tomorrow." When he returned, he brought ten pounds of bacon, a crate of corn, several cases of beer, some tonic water, and a bottle of gin.

For 15 summers, the boys and I met with Rankin family members at the Lake. We were disappointed when Pop announced they were selling. It had become too much work for them. Pop by then was in his late 70's, Mother, five years younger.

He lived another ten years. I asked him if he were afraid to die. "No," he answered, "but I don't want it to hurt." It didn't. He contracted Parkinson's Disease, hated becoming increasingly dependent, but never lost his sense of humor. One time while he was still eating at the dinner table, Mother motioned to Pop that he needed to wipe the side of his mouth. He did and commented, "I'm just like Pavlov's dogs. Ring the bell for dinner and I'll salivate."

He also kept his strong, alert, opinionated mind. When I told him I was joining the Great Peace March in 1986, he mumbled, "God damnedest dumbest thing I've ever heard of." I had his comment printed across the back of a sweatshirt and wore it while walking nine months across the United States. Those words were almost the last he spoke to me. He died in his sleep November 9, 1985.

When the medics came to take his body out the door, thunder roared in the pre-dawn skies. There was no rain. Just a reverberating clap of thunder. A week later, after the Memorial Service and Celebration, I stayed on with Mother for a while. My brother David was finishing a deck he'd been building for them. He called me outside one mid-morning and pointed up. "What do you see?" he asked. I saw a red-tail hawk hovering just above us. "What do you think?" David peered at me. "It's a hawk," I said. "What do you think? Do you think it's Pop still telling you what to do?" "Exactly" concluded David.

When I got home I opened my dictionary of symbols. A clap of thunder at the time of death means direct access into heaven. A hawk, although second to the eagle in importance, is a messenger from heaven. Pop had sent the hawk to David and me. Mother said she couldn't imagine Pop as a bird.

I never thought of him as a bird, but do think he has sent a red tail hawk more than once. I have seen them on fence posts while driving, trying to make an important decision. They have appeared on a telephone wire when I was troubled. Even now, in 2004, in Capitola, I live across the street from a tall cypress tree where each year a pair of hawks nest. A reminder from Pop. He's finally saying to me, "You done good, Sis.".

I Remember Ben

In 1935 when my parents moved from Fourth Street across town to 350 South Coulter Street (now Dean St) in Coquille, Oregon, I was a knobby-kneed, scrawny, shy-eyed eight-year-old third-grader with two younger brothers. John, shiny bright and curly, was in first grade. Our solemn, big-eyed brother Richard was only two. Youngest brother, David, would come when I was 10. On school mornings, Mother, her dark hair braided in a tight ridge across her head and wearing a fresh, ironed, flowered house dress, walked John and me the half block to Second Street. At the corner, she stood holding Richard's hand. They watched as we diminished up toward Washington Grade School. John and I, like most children, walked to school; only farm kids rode the bus.

By the time I was in Lincoln Junior High School, I had noticed Ben Barton. I knew he was a grade ahead of me and laughed a lot with a bunch of boys. As he strode past our house on the way to his home at the end of Coulter Street, he racketed a stick along our white picket fence. He was solid, strong-looking, with the build of a boy who would grow to play football. I thought him electric. Even his brown straight hair stood up, like a bristle of antennas. Mother looked out the window when he sauntered by. "That Ben!" she'd say and shake her head.

When a new girl, Diana Powers, moved into the immaculate stucco house across the street from the Barton's rambling brown shingle, John and I walked up to play with her and Albert, who was in John's grade. Their mother seemed always to be resting in their dim living room. Mother said the elegant Ruth Powers must have the vapors. John and I waited for Diana and Albert and watched the older boys swarming beneath the basketball hoop nailed to the power pole at the end of the street. Ben was one of them. I watched Tom Martin, Dave and Bob Kline, Jim Young, but mostly I watched Ben. His hair bounced as he caught the ball, shouldered a drive to the basket, and shot wildly. I silently cheered his score. Sometimes he'd grin over at John and me. Eventually we even got to play. As I grew taller than some of the boys, I became a good shooter. For a girl.

John entered Lincoln Junior High and Mother told me, "You walk with him until he gets used to going across town." One afternoon we were about a block from home, just passing the stone retaining wall across the street from Bobby Taylor's house. Ben was there, balancing along the top of the wall. Showing off. Making smart remarks. Suddenly he sprang down toward us. John fell to the ground with a thwack. Ben sat on him and my brother yowled. With wildcat fury I flew onto Ben's back, strangling him. Gasping, Ben rolled off and sat on the grass. John and I ran lickety-split down the hill, didn't even look right nor left at Second Street, galloped the half block to veer in through the gate and to the back yard. We scuttled into our clubhouse beneath the apple tree. Safe! Ben Barton never picked on John again.

One day a few years ago when John was approaching retirement age and our brother Richard had developed handsome grey at his temples, we sat together having a glass of wine. I asked John if he remembered the time Ben took him down. "No," he answered, "But do you remember when Charlie Walker and Ben found the spool of copper wire beneath the basketball hoop?"

"No. What happened?"

"They tied one end of the wire around the power pole and pushed a stick through the spool. Each one held an end of the stick, and shoulder-to-shoulder, they walked backward down Coulter Street, unreeling wire for a block and a half until they reached our house. We were sitting on the curb, writing in the gutter dust. Ben warned, 'Now, don't you two touch this wire! If you do, we'll come get you!' Then they walked on, crossing Second Street and disappearing beyond Bobby Taylor's house and up the hill past the mortuary."

"And." I asked, "What did we do?"

John chuckled, "We ran out and touched it! Don't you remember?"

"Then what happened? Did they come get us?"

"No, nothing happened. Mother called us in to dinner."

I didn't remember the copper wire, but I remembered one May Day very early in the morning when I slipped up Coulter Street and hung a purple construction-paper basket full of Mother's spring flowers on the brass door handle of the heavy oak door recessed beyond the shadows of the Barton's front porch. Then, with feet never touching the sidewalk, I fled back home and disappeared into to my room before Pop was up making coffee at his usual six o'clock."

Richard had been listening to John and me reminisce. He asked, "Remember when Ben used to come down and call 'ta-wit-ta-woo' and we all swarmed out to play after dinner? We played Kick-the-Can in the street. You older kids never did tell us younger ones what 'ta-wit-ta-woo' meant."

"I don't know what it meant," I poured us more wine. John leaned forward. "It meant 'I'm hiding in Schroeder's woodshed. Come and find me!'"

I laughed. "I bet you're right, John. But let me tell you about what I think Ben's best stunt was. The Great Dummy Caper. When we were teen-agers, Ben, Jim Young, Philip Clausen, Duane Mitchell and Jimmy Peart made a dummy by stuffing rags into a pair of cords and a Coquille High School letterman sweater. He wore a baseball cap. Ben propped the dummy up among the boys in a back booth at Brandon's. Remember Brandon's after school? Marianne Rackliff with her red curls fluttered about chirping, 'Who's the new boy in town!'"

"The following Friday night at the Liberty Theater, a fearsome scream echoed from the balcony. An adolescent voice shrieked, 'Suicide!' The dummy landed on startled people seated below. The movie reel stopped. The lights went up. Mr. Claver, owner of the Liberty, couldn't catch Ben and the others as they, with the dummy, escaped out the side exit. I sat awed by those boys, especially Ben."

John asked, "Did you have a crush on Ben?"

"No, I don't think so. I loved his daring, his original ideas, his enthusiasm for fun. I wished I could be more daring. Maybe I wished I could be a boy and do what he and his friends did."

By 1945 I was one of about fifteen Coquille students enrolled at the University of Oregon out in Eugene. Once in a while Ben and I rode home to Coquille in the same car. During those three-hour rides, Ben occupied himself by lobbing beer bottles out the window, over the car, at fence posts on the other side of the highway. I was impressed by his aim and grateful a responsible Wilbur Craig was driving. Sometimes we sang. Ben began by humming, then with a lusty voice, led us in rousing rounds of college songs.

It was Ben's idea that we college students go Christmas caroling. Wilbur had a flatbed truck. Beneath the deep December sky sprayed with frozen stars, about a dozen of us roamed across Coquille, singing all the way. When we got to Coulter Street, we trooped into our house and Mother served us hot cranberry punch.

I think it was Ben's idea that we enter a float in the All Roads Lead to Coquille 4th of July Celebration Parade. We decorated Wilbur's truck with banners, pennants and streamers. I volunteered our family's freezer to make root beer popsicles in ice-cube trays. In the parade, we swayed along, standing in the back of the truck tossing root beer popsicles to the crowds on the curbs of downtown. Ben named it The Root Beer Float.

The seasons flowed one into another. After University graduation, I married and moved down to California. Ben remained in Coquille with his father's title insurance business.

Following our father's memorial service in early December of 1985, I stood beside Mother on the steps of St. James Episcopal Church on Third Street in Coquille. Among the mourners paying respects to my mother, my brothers, and to me, I noticed a distinguished looking gentleman nattily dressed in grey slacks and blue blazer. He moved forward to murmur gently to Mother, "Mrs. Rankin, we all admired your husband and will miss him." Gravely he turned to me and with infinite tenderness, reached out his hand. He touched my arm and melted away. Before the next person approached, I turned to ask Mother, "Who was that?".

"Oh, Donna, didn't you recognize him? That was Ben Barton."

The Room Behind His Office

The room behind Pop's office was clean. Always clean. Squeaky clean. Smelled clean, looked clean, felt clean and crisp. It was antiseptic clean. White walls, white woodwork, stainless steel instruments arranged on white linen in a gleaming stainless steel tray. Glistening glass cabinet doors and jars. Folded white hand towels stacked on white shelves above a white sink with glittering faucets. Clean. It had to be. It was his examining room. My father was a doctor. He had his office and a small hospital in Coquille, a dairy and mill town of 4,000 people in a damp valley in southwestern Oregon.

I loved that room. It smelled like Pop smelled when he came home to dinner. His rough tweed jacket, his hug, and his hands. His surgeon's hands, long tapering fingers, short flat nails. Always clean.

Clean fingernails were important to my mother. When I dated Ben Dement in high school, Mother liked him. "He has clean nails." she summarized. I was dazzled by his basketball prowess, his mellow voice, his convertible, the way I felt when we danced together. Mother liked his fingernails. They were clean like Pop's. To her, clean fingernails meant a profession or at least not blue collar.

The room behind Pop's office was a place of mystery. I never knew what happened to others in that room, but I knew one thing. After lunch at Brandon's Cafe or with Dave Rackleff in the back of the pharmacy, Pop returned to his office, shushed the receptionist, alerted the nurses, went into his office and shut the door. He removed his shoes, sat up on the examining table, lay back and took a nap. "Twenty minutes," he declared. "That's all I need and then I'm good for the rest of the day." He had long days from about six in the morning until nine or ten at night, plus deliveries. His nap was an open secret. No one disturbed him as he rested in that clean, white room.

One spring after dinner when I was seven and brother John almost six, I said, "I'll make an arrow for you. I know how." I brought a kitchen knife out to the back porch, stood a piece of kindling wood on the chopping block and began to slice down the clear white cedar. The knife slipped and I sliced my thumb. John ran to find Mother. "Donna's bleeding a little. Not much. Better bring a big towel." She did and called my father from the living room where he sat reading.

He didn't say much, just unwrapped the towel, wrapped another smaller one tightly, bundled me into the car and drove the few blocks to his office in the Coquille Hospital. He herded me through the waiting room, through his office and into the clean, white room behind. After he lifted me up to sit on the examining table, he took a silver dollar out of his pocket and placed it nearby. "Now, Sis, if you hold still while I stitch your thumb, you may have that dollar. Just keep looking at it. This will hurt a little and it's ok to cry, but don't move."

I had never had a whole silver dollar. I kept my eye on it and jerked only a little when I felt the poke of the novocain needle. After four stitches, he bandaged my hand, lifted me down off the table and gave me the dollar.

Seventy years and that's the best dollar I ever earned. And I still love the stringent fragrance of antiseptic....white and shiny. Clean. Like the room behind his office. Like my father.

The Day We Lost Sam

On the day after Thanksgiving in 1956, Santa Claus was to land in a helicopter in the parking lot behind Byron's Shoe Store in San Mateo, California. I didn't know, as I dressed our young sons to go see him, that the day would be one of stark terror.

At three-and-a-half, Matt knew the routine. He saw me coming with his red, white and blue train sweater, braced himself on sturdy legs, and raised his arms. Sam, two-and-a-half, took his sweater from me.

"I do it," he stated. And couldn't. "You do it," and raised his arms, his dark eyes full of trust. John, who had celebrated his first birthday in September, clenched his face shut while I pulled his sweater down over his blond head. Three little boys in matching train sweaters knitted for them by their Grandmother Love.

Matt climbed into the double stroller and tugged on Sam as he grunted in. I tucked John into the basket behind his brothers and we began the mile-long adventure toward downtown. After a while Matt climbed out to help push and John sat beside Sam to eat Cheerios. A clown stood at the corner of Third and Ellsworth and handed out balloons. I tied them to the boys' wrists. We were pushing through the crowds when the helicopter appeared overhead.

"There's Santa!" Matt, his taffy curls glinting in the pale sunlight, pointed upward.

"There's Santa!" Sam echoed as he squinted and pointed. John sucked his fingers and tilted his face skyward.

"Now, boys, be sure you stay with me. We'll get close to Santa Claus." My hand over Matt's, we skirted the edge of the crowed toward an opening. "Excuse me. Excuse me. May we get through?"

I stretched up to get a better view. Forged ahead. Checked the boys. Sam was gone. He was just gone!

"Matt," I commanded." Get into the stroller. Hold John's hand. You two must stay in the stroller!" Frantic, I scanned the crowd and shouted, "Sam! Sam!"

Tell Me a Story

I couldn't watch Matt and John and search for Sam at the same time, so pushed the stroller into Byron's Shoe Store where we were well known. Mr. Harris came smiling toward us. "Yes, Mrs. Love, the boys need shoes again so soon?"

"No, Mr. Harris. But I need your help. We've lost Sam."

"Oh, my. Here, let me." He steered the stroller toward the cashier and said to her, "You keep these boys safe while I help find Sam." I handed her the Cheerios.

Mr. Harris took my arm and guided me out the door. "You look around that way and I'll search over there. I'll stop by your husband's office to ask him to come help."

Every little boy in a red, white and blue-sweater might have been Sam and wasn't. I circled around and met Mr. Harris.

He reported, "Mr. Love has gone to the police station. Maybe Sam's been turned in."

Panicked thoughts raced through my head. Maybe he's been stolen. Maybe he's been run over. He's probably as terrified as I am. Oh, Dear God, please help us find Sam!

Mr. Harris took me back to Matt and John. I wiped John's face and sat down. The customer in the next chair continued trying on black oxfords. Matt sat on my lap and asked, "After Sam comes back can we go see Santa Claus?"

I didn't want him to see my tears so I clutched him tight to me. John dozed. We were like that when their father came in with Sam in his arms. They had matching smiles. Sam had a sucker.

Jim said, "The officer told me a woman brought him in. She was waiting at the cross walk for the green light on El Camino. When Sam stepped from the curb, she grabbed his shoulder and asked him where he as going. Sam looked up at her and in all seriousness, told her, 'Home.' The woman took his hand, said, 'I'll help you,' and walked him to the police station. When I got there, Sam was sitting on a desk enjoying the attention. I wish I knew who she was. Who was that masked man?" he joked.

Mr. Harris came over to beam at the boys and shake Jim's hand. Matt wiggled to make room on my lap for his brother and Jim handed him down. I didn't care now if the whole world saw my tears.

"Do you want to go see Santa Claus, Mommy?" Matt, his blue eyes full of concern, patted my chest.

I hugged them both to me and stroked Matt as I faced Sam and his sticky sucker, "You, my wanderer, must stay with me. You went away and I was scared. Were you scared?"

"No."

"Did you cry?"

"Yes."

"Why?"

"I lost my balloon."

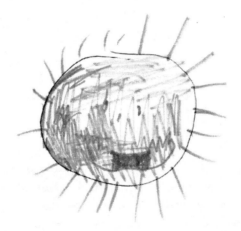

Our Very Own Second Grade Drop-out

Our youngest son Marty was seven, in the second grade, when he dropped out of school. I hadn't even known he was unhappy. Each morning his older brothers, in the fourth, fifth, and sixth grades, rode their bikes out the driveway to school and Marty walked. I thought he chose to walk.

Then, one Monday morning, after they'd all gone off with their books and brown bag lunches – tuna sandwiches, apples, chips, celery, a cookie – I went out to the station wagon to do errands and there was Marty, lying in the back, looking at a book.

"What are you doing?" I asked. "I thought you'd left for school."

"I'm not going to school any more." He barely looked up. His light brown hair flopped over his forehead and shadowed his deep blue eyes. I smiled to myself and thought, now I'd have a chance to be with Marty alone, a rare occasion in our busy family.

"Oh. Well, you'd better come with me to do the marketing."

He brightened and scrambled up to the front seat. He flashed a look at me and failed to repress a wide, snaggle-toothed grin. I asked him what he wanted to do.

"I want to stay home. I'm not learning anything. I could learn more at home."

"Like what?"

"I could learn Chinese from Chris." Chris Chiu was a college student from Hong Kong who lived with us. "I could learn to count in Chinese. They don't teach us that at North School."

"You sound as though you've given this some thought," I patted his knee. "All right, you may stay home, learn Chinese and read books. But there will be no TV. You can practice writing by writing letters to your grandmothers. Agreed?"

He looked like he'd won a major battle. Not as hard as he'd thought it would be. Tuesday, he stayed home from school. He and Chris spent time up in the tree house and Marty came down rattling off Chinese. His letter to Grandmother Rankin included a picture of Chris. Wednesday morning he practiced his guitar and shot baskets by himself. By Wednesday afternoon, he was wandering around waiting for his brothers to get home.

Thursday morning, we went for a walk and I asked, "Are you sure you want to stay home? What about giving school another chance?"

"Ok," he looked serious. "But I want to be in the third grade."

"Hmm. Let's go speak to the principal to see what he says. Mr. Brown is pretty understanding." We turned toward North School.

Mr. Brown, a big bear of a man, came around from behind his desk and bent down to shake hands with Marty. I explained Marty's desire to be in third grade and Mr. Brown offered, "Ok. We can give you a test to see if you're ready. If you are, we'll just move you up a grade. But today, you must return to your classroom. It's only mid-morning, so you can go now."

Marty's eyes glazed over. His lower lip protruded just like my brother John's and Mother had called him mule stubborn. I was surprised when Marty got up and went out the door without saying goodbye. I wasn't surprised to see him running out around the flagpole, across the baseball diamond, and through the gate toward home. Mr. Brown and I shrugged and I promised that Marty would be in school next week.

When I returned home and climbed through the hole in the back fence, I found him up in the tree house. "Come down. We have to talk again."

"Is Mr. Brown mad?"

"No, but he thinks you should be in school. You can take the test tomorrow."

He held onto the rope ladder, "I'll flunk it. They won't let me in third grade. I don't know enough, but I'm big enough to ride my bike and Mr. Brown won't let second graders ride. I can ride just as good as Matt and Sam and John. They get to ride and I have to walk all by myself." Tears glistened. He looked away.

"Is that what you want? You want to ride your bike to school?" I hugged him to me and felt tears in my own eyes. "You had lots of courage to drop out of school because you wanted to ride

Tell Me a Story

your bike with your brothers. That was a hard way to do it. We'll think of something."

He sniffed and rubbed his nose across my shoulder. "Well, Matt won't walk with me. I know that."

As his brothers swarmed into the kitchen for after-school snacks, Marty sat with his face practically buried in his milk glass. I explained the problem. Sam offered, "We could take turns walking with him in the mornings, but what about after school?" John said, "Well, he has friends, doesn't he? Don't you have friends to walk home with, Marty?"

"Sure. I have Bobby and Lisa and lots more. I already walk home with them." He looked sideways at Matt who nodded and folded the paper to the comics. John marked the schedule on the calendar.

The next morning, Friday, as I handed out the lunches, Matt smiled and nudged Marty, "Come on, Bro. Let's go."

Deedle Deedle Dumpling, My Son John

By the time our third son John came along, I knew how. I knew how to have a baby and feel pampered at the same time. Jim and I adopted our first son. That was easy. Well, almost easy. We had little preparation time. No parenting classes. Just Pop's calling from Coquille, Oregon, on an August Monday in 1953 to say, "I found one." Tuesday morning Jim drove me from our home on Hobart Street in San Mateo to the San Francisco Airport. In the newsstand there I bought Dr Spock's Baby Book to read on the two-hour flight to North Bend in Southwestern Oregon. Mother met me and we stopped in at The Hub to buy baby supplies. An hour later I was holding the blue bundle, the boy Jim and I named Matthew, Gift from God. Instant motherhood. "Kind of overwhelming, isn't it? Better sit down." Pop advised.

Eight and half months later, Sam was born. During pregnancy I had learned what I could about natural childbirth. I knew how to breathe. Jim checked me into Mills Hospital in San Mateo a little before one o'clock Monday morning, May 3, 1954. Intermittent labor continued until early Tuesday morning. At four o'clock, my OB, Dick Morrison, announced, "You're getting tired, Donna, and so is the baby. Let's do a C-section". Sam was gorgeous even with a tiered forehead. Jim said, "His head looks like the steppes of China."

In August of 1955, Dick Morrison said I could choose the birth date this time. Either September 20 or 27 would be safe for the baby. I marked September 20 on the calendar. The child's birthday parties could be on the 20th and the next day the children could eat leftovers while Jim took me out for my own birthday dinner.

As the due date approached, I stocked the house with groceries, extra laundry detergent, and paper goods, and called the diaper service. Charlie, the milkman for Berkeley Farms delivered. Three times a week, he came into the kitchen, checked the milk, cheese, and ice cream supplies and left what we needed. I wrote a note introducing Jim's mother who would be caring for Matt and Sam and posted it on the refrigerator for Charlie. Frozen homemade dinners were ready as well as a stack of waffles to be heated in the toaster.

I made appointments for Monday, September 19. "I'd like to have my hair done, and have a manicure and pedicure. No polish, though. I'm having a baby tomorrow and they need to be able to see the color of my nails." Late that afternoon, I checked into Mills Hospital and enjoyed a quiet dinner in bed. In the evening Jim brought Matt and Sam to stand on the hospital lawn and wave up at me in the window. They were so young! Matt had just had his second birthday in August and Sam was 16 months old. I prayed the new baby would be as healthy as the two down there with their father.

Tuesday morning before eight, I was wheeled into surgery. Soon "Another boy, Donna," Dick called out. "Going to name this one Luke? How about Luke Love?" Sounded like a hiccup! Later that day I held our new son. He was a serene baby with long fingers, big feet and two cowlicks swirling his blond fuzz. I examined him closely and knew him to be perfect.

I handed the baby back to the nurse and ordered the San Francisco Chronicle delivered to my room along with two pots of tea. Every morning for the 10 days I was in the hospital, I dawdled over breakfast. The orange slices, lying in a concentric circle on their own plate, were juicy, elegant, transparently thin. I sipped tea and read the paper. I read the cards and admired the flowers that arrived. I asked for a foot rub. I took long uninterrupted showers. Of course, my belly felt as though it might fall to the floor, but I held it with my hands and it didn't.

When Jim came after work, we talked about names. "Your turn," he said. "I did Sam for my grandfather."

I didn't hesitate. " Let's name him for Pop. John. John Rankin Love. How does that sound?"

"Great!" Jim agreed.

"Pop'll be pleased. He'll know how much we honor him."

John was four days old when Pop, followed by Mother, blasted into the room. His rangy 6' 2" frame filled the doorway. The Harris-tweed jacket rumpled, pockets lumpy, camera swinging from his shoulder. "Ah, here you are! And the baby here, too. Good timing. What do you think, Ma?" he turned to Mother. "Don't call me Ma!"

Tell Me a Story

she commanded, then came around to look closely at me, touched my shoulder. "You look tired, Sis."

Pop pulled a chair over close to the bed, but instead of sitting down, he climbed up and stepped onto the bed. Standing astride my legs, he took out his camera. "Unwrap the baby a little." Flash bulbs popped. "Look up more, Donna." More flashes. A nurse entered. "Sir! Get down this instant! You can't be up there." Pop fumbled with another flashcube, "It's all right," he said. "I'm a doctor." Mother and I exchanged amused glances. "That's your father." she shrugged. John was calm throughout, just lying in my arms, in his family, in his new world.

Pop was entirely pleased with his namesake, his third grandson. He smiled down at me, "You done good, Sis." He expressed concern for me. "You'll be very busy, day and night," he said. The next day he pushed open the door, came to the bedside without his usual gusto and offered me a package. It was Anne Morrow Lindberg's Gift From the Sea. "You might find a little time to read this." I started as soon as he left.

All these years and I still have that book. During active motherhood it reminded me to pace myself, that a woman needs to go to her own well for refreshment in order to serve others. Whenever I give a copy to a young woman, I think of those 10 days when I first met John.

⸙

John was a mellow infant. He slept, ate and slept. However, noise distracted him. In the evenings Matt and Sam had quiet playtime with Jim while I fed John in the kitchen with the door closed. During the middle of the night feedings, I bathed him and we had our own uninterrupted times together. When he was crawling and things got noisy, he climbed up into any lap, leaned back, stuck two fingers in his mouth and one in his nose, and gazed off into space.

He was a child we all cared for. Sam brought him breakfast in bed. He emptied an entire box of Cheerios into the crib and added a peeled banana. When I got to his room, John sat squishing the banana through his fingers. Cheerios were stuck to his hands and face. He looked up and wiggled with pleasure.

Matt, the boy who before he could walk, had fetched diapers in his mouth for Sam, now pushed a chair over to climb up and open the refrigerator door. He reached in for three baby bottles of milk. One for Sam, one for John, and one for himself.

Eighteen months after John's birth, the next child was due. At dinner one night Jim and I asked the boys, "If this next baby is another boy, what shall we name him?" We weren't surprised when they suggested one of the heroes in a favorite Walt Disney program. Each late afternoon, Matt, Sam and John lined their little red chairs in front of the TV, put on their Mickey Mouse hats and sat transfixed by "The Adventures of Spin and Marty." So when Matt and Sam at once voted, "Spin!", we laughed. Jim vetoed that.

They all shouted," Marty!"

"Let me have one of your business cards," I asked Jim. Across the back I printed Martin Taylor Love. Taylor is my mother's maiden name. It looked fine, had dignity. Later, Jim and I realized that we had given the first and fourth boys identical initials, confusing when labeling socks and underwear, but what's more, they say M T Love, empty love.

When John was about two and Sam three, Sam taught John to use the toilet. Sam demonstrated, John copied. But he was too short and he missed. John then stood on Sam's feet while he aimed. We found a little stool for John to stand on and be independent.

When they were five, four, and three, Matt, Sam and John were car-pooled week-day mornings to St. Matthew's Episcopal Day School at Baldwin and El Camino in San Mateo. One noon, Marty and I pulled up to the curb and the children piled into the car. I took all of them home to our house to lunch. I scattered raisins on the kitchen table and slathered rows of bread slices with peanut butter and honey. "Matt," I asked, "will you go get John and tell him to wash his hands? He's probably in his room." Matt came back, "He's not there," and slid into his chair. I looked out the back door to the swing set, on the sofa where John sometimes dozed off, and out along the curb. Sandwich quarters sat on paper napkins in front of each child. Sam stopped chewing long enough to say, "He wasn't in the car." Oh. "Ok, everyone, bring your sandwich, get back into the car. No, not you, Duffer. Dogs stay home." All the six miles back to school, I prayed, "Please, God, keep John safe. Please, God, I know I'm a terrible mother. Please."

As we pulled closer to school, there was John sitting on the curb, leaning against a tree, two fingers in his mouth and one in his nose. I leapt out to hug him and tell him I was so sorry. I cried. He melted into me and mumbled, "I knew you'd come back." Matt gave him the crust of his sandwich.

The boys went through childhood in a herd. "The Love Boys." Their father and I made every effort to remember their individualities, but usually within the context of the group. John was quiet, undemanding, agreeable. Often he disappeared upstairs to his room to work quietly on a model or puzzle. He was organized. In the mornings, he'd slither out of bed, hardly rumpling the covers, go into the bathroom to turn on the water and while it got warm, he got dressed. Then he washed. On his way downstairs, he brought the laundry hamper from the boys' bathroom. He was about six the morning he came through the kitchen to empty the hamper in the laundry room, came back through to leave the basket at the bottom of the back stairway, returned and stood in the middle of the kitchen. He didn't move, just stood there. I asked, "What is it, John?" "Hmmm," he squinted in thought, "what was I going to do next?" I hugged him. "Breakfast?" "Oh, yeah, that's it! Breakfast!" and he sat at his place.

By 1961, Sam, seven, was taking piano lessons from Mrs. Lawson in her home. John came along so he and I could read together while Sam had his lesson. Sam was to practice each morning before breakfast. One morning I stopped stirring the eggs and rounded the corner into the music room to say, "Sam, you are doing really well on that piece!" It wasn't Sam at all. It was John! We took Sam off piano and put John on.

North Hillsborough Grade School offered music lessons as well as some instruments. Matt already was playing their trombone. I told Sam, "You choose anything you want to play but whatever it is, you must stick with it a year. Then you can change your mind if you wish." At school, in second grade, Sam pointed to the picture, thinking it was a guitar. It was a violin. For a year before breakfast, Sam sawed away, Matt blew his horn, and John played piano. The next year, Sam started guitar lessons. Matt continued to play trombone and joined the chorus in Crocker Middle School. John continued to play piano as well as the drums Sam bought the Saturday after I'd said, "Any mother who would allow a drum set in the house has to be crazy!" Marty played the drums, too, as well as guitar. Our home was full of music!

Good breakfasts were important to me. Always juice, fruit and milk. Hot cereal during the week and on Saturdays, pancakes, eggs, bacon. One Saturday I slept in and wakened to the fragrance of pancakes and syrup. Guiltily I went down to the kitchen. John, a good reader in Third Grade, had climbed up to get the Bisquick Box, read the directions, plugged in the griddle, and was making pancakes for himself and his brothers. A new tradition had begun.

John was nine. In 1964 Elizabeth Vargas, a student at College of San Mateo, lived with our family in the house on Brewer Drive in Hillsborough. With her usual sparkling enthusiasm, she was planning a summertime visit to her family in San Salvador and invited any one of our sons to go with her. Matt, eleven, said, "I'll go if Sam goes." Sam said, "I want to go to Boy Scout camp." I looked at John. He was wan and didn't eat very well. Assertive seven-year-old Marty piped up, "I'll go." For days he was excited and then at dinner one evening, Elizabeth had said, "Marty, eat your beans. We have them every day."

Marty had poured milk, looked down, and announced, "I'm not going." Next day I moaned to my authoritative friend Sally. Waving her hands emphatically, she replied, "So? What's your problem? John doesn't eat in San Salvador? He doesn't eat at home. Let him go. It's too good an opportunity to miss." When I talked with him, John peered brightly through his glasses, tugged at his left ear, and replied, "I didn't know why you wouldn't let me go. I can learn to like beans."

I believed him. Together we packed his bag.

They were gone five weeks. When I met them at the San Francisco airport, John was pale beneath his woven tropical hat, but was rounder, even had a little tummy. Elizabeth, with her arm around his shoulders, explained, "My mother was afraid he would get sunburned so had him play under the wharf at the estero. He and my brother Pepe went to the beach almost every day. They became good friends and only once had an argument."

John added, "Pepe wanted to watch Popeye on TV and I wanted to watch Spanish cartoons. And, Mom, you should see the butterflies! I should have taken my butterfly net. They have tons of butterflies." Without stopping for breath, he continued, "Everyone rubbed my hair. They kept saying 'oro, oro.' And guess what! Señora Vargas fixed hamburguesas and spaghetti 'cause she knew I liked them.

John was no longer a quiet retiring boy. He had something to say. He became our expert on Central America, got easy A's in Spanish classes, and most of the time ate his beans.

※

As the boys grew, music remained important to them. All four played in school bands and orchestras. Sam and John formed a Dixieland Band with some friends. They became good enough to play several charity parties. As adults, they still play and sing.

Jim had joined me when I encouraged the boys in music. He also said, "Choose a sport. I don't care what it is, but choose something." In the 1960's Matt played tennis and for a while was the only white boy on the San Mateo High School basketball team. From the sidelines, I shouted, "Give the ball to Matt! Give the ball to Matt!" Sam, John and Marty went out for Cross Country running and Spring track. I had a busy time in the bleachers rooting for them, especially when they were competing in the same race. They all told me, "Mom, you have to sit quietly. You can't yell so much!"

Matt was at Yale and Sam at University of Oregon, when John was a senior in high school. One Saturday morning he spread a map of the United States across the breakfast table and muttered to himself, "Not New England. Matt's there. Not the Northwest. Hmmm, South or Midwest." He opened the College Directory.

"Ok, Mom, college is the time for the Love Boys to spread out. How about Duke? Or Northwestern in Evanston? They both have good music and math departments." He applied and eventually chose Northwestern, majored in computer science, pledged a fraternity and played triple drums in the marching band. I have always regretted saying no when he phoned to ask me to come to Evanston one November to watch him play. I could have found the money and time, but didn't. I learned from that to refuse the boys' invitations only when absolutely necessary.

During the boys' growing up years their friends had come to our house to play. We didn't have a pool like many had. We had a large level back yard, climbing trees, and half a basketball court. Of course, there were girls. Girls came to watch Sam work on his Morris Minors. Some came to shoot baskets. Or just be there. During junior and senior years, Dora and John dated. She was a quiet, modest daughter of a proper Japanese family. She played first flute in the high school band. John, tall now, sensitive and considerate, came to stand beside me one afternoon as I stirred something on the stove. "Mom, can I make an appointment with you to talk?" In an hour we met in the sunroom, put up a Do Not Disturb sign and closed the doors.

"Ok, John, what is it?"

He fiddled with his hands a moment and then looked up with such intensity that I wanted to gather him right up onto my lap...all 6'2" of him. "It's Dora."

"Yes?" I held my breath. Was this the announcement all parents feared?

"Well, she wants to go steady and I'm going away to college and don't want to even think of going steady. It was fine during high school, but now things will change. Will you talk to her?"

"Yes! Yes, John, I will. Bring her over, wait a minute, let me get the calendar, bring her over, how about Saturday morning?" She came and we three sat together on the patio while I talked and Dora cried. John sat close to her and listened.

In September 1973, John packed his trunk and flew to Chicago. He called to say he'd got a ride to Evanston and was getting settled into the dorm. "But, Mom, could you send some chopsticks? On the weekends dinners are not served so I bought a hotplate and a pan. I can do a stir fry but Evanston doesn't have any chopsticks!"

Tell Me a Story

It's Been Quite A Day!

March 10, 1971, dawned in Hillsborough, California, like any other spring day. Damp, not wet. My husband Jim, in his middle-forties, looking as crisp as when we met in 1948 at the University of Oregon, commuted, as usual, before full daylight, to the office in San Francisco. About eight o'clock, our three older sons, Matt, Sam, and John, rode their bikes to San Mateo High School. The youngest, Marty, rode his the opposite direction to Crocker Middle School. They had their brown bag lunches. I was going to the dentist.

Jim's cousin Helen, "Hand-wringing-Helen," at her best when needed, arrived to accompany me. At age forty-two, I was getting the last wisdom tooth pulled and had been instructed by the oral surgeon, "Get someone to drive you."

Helen waited in the reception room as the tooth was removed and returned us safely home. Good, there in the driveway was the Izmirian Furnace Company's truck.

"They're replacing the old furnace today," I mumbled around the cotton packing in my mouth. "Look at all that scrap iron flying out the basement door!" Hunks landed and sprayed gravel. The decorated cast iron furnace door flew out.

"What beautiful scroll designs on the door!" I pointed out to Helen. Then I wondered aloud, "Why is Jim's car here? What is Jim doing home? I guess he's getting ready to go to the junior partners' meeting in New York. Is that the director's chair folded against the bumper? The boys and I gave that to him for Christmas. Maybe it's a prop for a skit. Strange, though, I thought he was going tomorrow. I'll go upstairs to find out."

Helen worried, "Maybe his mother is ill and he's going to see her. You go find out. Bring the ice bag to put on your jaw. I'll make some tea." She walked toward the kitchen.

Upstairs I stretched to hug my energetic ectomorphic husband.

"Everything ok?" I asked. "Have you seen the ice bag? I thought you were going to New York tomorrow."

He corrected me, "I'm leaving today."

"Oh, ok." I rummaged through the shelves in our bathroom. "Haven't you seen the ice bag?" and opened the door to a hall closet. Jim trailed along behind me, his hands full of socks. I headed for the boys' bathroom. "I'm leaving today," he repeated.

I reached behind a stack of towels beneath the washbowl and found the ice bag. "Oh. I guess I just misunderstood."

"No," Jim looked at his socks. "Tomorrow I'm going to New York. Today I'm moving out and going to live in a townhouse down at Woodlake."

Stunned, I could only utter, "Oh." Woodlake is where all the local separated husbands go, I thought.

"Do you want to talk about it?" he asked.

"No! I don't want to talk about it! At least, not now. I'm going downstairs to get some ice and talk with Helen."

"Don't tell Helen!" he commanded as he disappeared back into his dressing room.

Helen filled the ice bag, took one look at me, and ordered, "Sit down. Something's seriously wrong. Do you want me to call your mother?"

"No! Don't call my mother!" The furnace men were making such a din in the basement directly beneath the kitchen table where we sat that she had difficulty hearing me. I was clutching the ice bag to my face.

She was wringing her hands. "Actually, Helen," I muttered, "thank you for driving me this morning. I don't mean to be abrupt, but I'll call you tomorrow." We heard Jim stamping up and down the stairs as he loaded his car.

Then I was alone. For an hour or so before the boys came home, I languished in our dim bedroom, numb jaw and numb mind. My most profound decision was, "In a while I'll order pizza for the boys' dinner." About four o'clock, they infused life back into the house. They thundered up the stairs and flowed into our bedroom.

Ranged around the foot of the bed, tall, slender, blond, eager; in many ways so like their father. Matt had had his wisdom teeth pulled only last year. He bent to check the ice supply. Sam, his tender heart in his eyes, touched my toes and looked concerned. John offered to refill the water glass.

Marty, wide-open and bouncy, said, "I'll get you Dad's radio. You can listen to some of your favorite music." He disappeared into Jim's dressing room. We heard drawers and doors opening and shutting. He reappeared, empty-handed, his face pale behind the scattering of freckles.

"What's happened to Dad?" It was a scream.

"Well." I inhaled, held it, and let it out. "I wasn't going to say anything until dinnertime, but..." and rushed into "Dad loves you very much! It has nothing to do with you! He's overtired. He needs to be alone. He's moved to Woodlake." I felt I had done it badly. First I'd failed Jim and now our sons.

"Oh" Marty sighed. "Is that all? I thought he was dead. Sam, you go get Mom your radio."

They melted away into their rooms. I determined to have a full discussion at dinner. No more holding back in this family. From now on we would open the way to full healthy communication. I got up, wandered around the house, sat at the kitchen table and stared out the window. I hardly heard my good friend Elaine Cunningham come in through the door.

"Hi!" she glided toward me. "I came to get the Auxiliary membership list." She stopped. "What's going on here? What's happened to you?" Her amber eyes glowed with compassion.

I told her. She reached over to tenderly pat my hand and in her slow Dallas drawl, summarized, "Well, my dear, it's been quite a day. You lost you' ol' fu'nace, you lost you' ol' tooth, and you lost you' ol' husband."

Feet

"This child will never walk," the delivering doctor told my mother. They both looked at my tiny newborn feet as they bent up with toes almost touching the shinbones. Mother looked him in the eye, and retorted, "You wanta bet?"

I was born at Emmanuel Hospital in Portland, Oregon, September 21, 1927. My father had taken my mother on the train to Portland and returned to Pendleton, unable to leave his internship at Eastern Oregon State Mental Institution. After 10 days in the hospital, Mother rested at her parents' home out in the Ivanhoe District of Portland. Grandmother and Grandfather Taylor later walked Mother and me the few blocks to the train. We could ride free because Grandfather Taylor worked for Southern Pacific. In the apartment in Pendleton, Mother held me on her lap to massage my feet down.

At the six months check-up, a doctor said, "Take this girl home and feed her mashed potatoes and gravy. She needs to gain weight." I wish I knew what he said about my feet. Mother continued massaging for over a year.

I walked late. At 15 months, but I walked. Early photos show me active and normal, playing with brother John, born May 30, 1929.

When Mother, Pop, John and I moved to Coos County, Mother shopped at the "largest department store in southwestern Oregon", the Hub, in Marshfield. There were no corrective shoes for my long, narrow, flexible, pronated feet. The best the salesman could do was carefully fit me into sturdy, brown, lace-up Girl Scout oxfords. Then he'd help me step up onto the platform of the mysterious machine standing at one side of the shoe department. I'd stick my feet into the openings and peer down through a viewing cone on top. The salesman pushed a button and we could see the bones of my feet within the shoes! A shoe-fitting machine! John and I took turns viewing our feet while Mother was distracted. I wore clunky Girl Scout shoes until I was twelve. I never got to wear shiny Mary Janes. In high school, college, and beyond, I wore Spalding saddle shoes just like everyone else and no longer felt like an Ugly

Duckling. Once in a while during teen-age years, for special dress-up occasions, I was allowed black platform sling pumps.

During the early 1940's our country was in World War II and I was in high school. Good shoe leather went to the military services. I attended boarding school at St. Helen's Hall in Portland, and Mother wrote letters admonishing, "Don't get your shoes wet!" As we girls walked the few blocks through the rain to the symphony, I took off my black sling pumps with cardboard soles and put them into my pockets. Only years later did I realize Mother meant to keep my feet dry, to stay healthy, that she was concerned and loved me. It wasn't the shoes, it was my feet. It was me!

After St. Helen's Hall and the University of Oregon, I married, moved to California, lived a typical 1950's suburban housewife life, mothered four sons, (two of whom wore corrective shoes), divorced, and grew up. In 1985 I was traveling with an American study group in Greece. One of the women and I hiked through a dusty, ancient olive grove below Delphi. She said, "I notice you like to walk. Let me tell you about a walk I'm going to take next year." As she spoke, I knew I would go, too. I didn't know how but I would. Connie was joining The Great Peace March to walk from Los Angeles to New York and down to Washington, DC. A planned Hollywood extravaganza of 12,000 on a glitzy, high profile demonstration for Global Nuclear Disarmament. Nine months camping across the country in colorful gumdrop tents. Walking 15 or more miles a day.

I signed up. The local San Mateo Times asked me to write feature stories as we progressed across the country. I had to report that the March was different from the initial plan. It was not glamorous, but it was everything else! In one article, written for Mother's Day, I gave credit to Mother for having massaged my feet down. For making this epoch in my life possible. When people along our Great Peace March route proclaimed, "You'll never make it", I told the story of one woman's determination to change a doctor's prognosis. I waved my arm to include all of us walkers and answered, "You wanta bet?"

It's In the Bag!

I took a flight from San Francisco to Los Angeles on February 14, 1986, because that was the only day Lynn Andrews could see us. My friend Connie, who lived in Los Angeles, was waiting for me at LAX. She paced on her sturdy hiker's legs, her mouth tight with anxiety. She'd had her dark, curly hair cut short. Her eyes sparked.

She hugged me. "I'm glad you're here! I'm so anxious to begin! I worried that you might not make it"

I had made it and felt centered. Excited, but focused. I didn't know how excited until a voice over the loudspeaker told Donna Love to report to lost and found, where the attendant handed me the word processor I was to use for reports back to the San Mateo Times. It had been found on a drinking fountain near the baggage carousal.

In two weeks, Connie and I, both in our late 50's, were joining the Great Peace March for Global Nuclear Disarmament. We were going to walk across the United States to wake up America to the threat of nuclear annihilation. Today we were going to see Lynn Andrews because both of us had read her book, Medicine Woman, and wanted to spend an hour with the author.

At one o'clock that Friday, we stood at the entrance to Lynn's home, a low rambling stone and beam structure. She met us at the door. The interior was hung with American Indian artifacts and smelled of fireplace smoke. It was duskier than a teepee. Lynn, an authority on North American Indian healing traditions, greeted us with a calm assurance and grace which was reassuring since the photo on the dust jacket of her book showed a cute, fluffy, curly Hollywood blond. She offered us mugs of tea and we settled into deep couches covered with fine Navajo rugs.

After introductory explanations about the impending Peace March in which thousands of people were to be walking from Los Angeles to Washington, DC, Connie asked, "What can you suggest we do when the Peace March gets difficult?"

Lynn cradled her mug of aromatic tea in both hands, leaned forward and said, "Get a totem."

"A totem?" I was puzzled. "What's a totem?"

She explained, "A totem is a spirit animal. Indians in both American continents have rites in which an animal appears as a guide. You two can watch your dreams for an animal or you can just think of animals until one feels right. Make yourselves small red cotton bags to hang around your necks. Put into them some sage, maybe a special small stone, and the fur of your totem animal. When you are exhausted, become that animal."

As soon as we left, Connie said her totem was a female mountain lion. I thought maybe a bear. It's brown, earthy, motherly. Also it's awkward and round, close to the ground. I needed an animal whose motions I could imagine, could emulate. Long legs, erect posture, good eyes. How about a giraffe? It has a 25-pound heart, is a vegetarian and can see far distances. Yes, a giraffe.

Connie knew a fabric store. We bought an eighth of a yard of excellent red cotton and found a friend with a sewing machine. Now, to get the fur. During the last week in February, the Peace March was camped in Griffith Park, just around the corner from the Los Angeles Zoo. Connie and I strolled over to the giraffe enclosure. No way to reach even a strand of air-born hair. Same with the mountain lion. We found the office of the Zoo Director. He was out, but his officious secretary assured us she would ask the director in the morning. I knew by her manner that there was only a slim chance we'd get bits of mountain lion and giraffe fur.

Next morning, her closed face told us the answer. I offered, "I know this is an unusual request, but this is an unusual cause."

"Oh, no, you're quite wrong," she contradicted. "We have American Indians in here all the time asking for hanks of hair and bits of fur. We can't accommodate them all." With an antiseptic grimace, she dashed our hopes with, "Anyway, disease can be spread that way." Now what would we do? There had to be a solution!

The following day Connie and I were doing a few errands along Melrose Avenue. At an open door, a paunchy furrier lounged against the wall, smoking in the sunshine. I saw behind him, beneath a cutting table, scraps of fur.

I smiled and appealed to him, "Do you have any very small scraps of fur we might have?"

He squinted and shook his head.

I pointed, "Just a handful from those beneath the table?"

"Oh, those! Sure! Much as you want!" He offered a shoebox. We filled it, thanked him, and took it to the nearest street bench.

"Sit down, Connie," I said. "I am going to find your piece of mountain lion fur." I pawed through the scraps and chose a pale one. "Here. This is it. This is mountain lion fur."

She looked skeptical. "How can you tell?"

"Trust me. This is it. And, now, you choose a piece of giraffe fur."

She rummaged a little while, picking up and discarding pieces. Finally, "Here. This is a piece of a dark spot from a Rothchilde giraffe."

"Looks like mink to me," I countered, but put it into the red cotton bag. She followed suit. We left the box of fur scraps on the bench for someone to discover. Maybe an American Indian on a totem search.

A few days later, as we idled in our small, rosy, dome tent, I dug the bit of fur from my totem bag. Still looked like mink.

"Come with me," Connie invited. "Let's go back to the zoo." I followed her through the gate and into the gift shop. She wandered away and then returned. Her face had the bright look of discovery. "Let me have your bag." From it, she took the bit of dark soft fur and attached a tiny enameled giraffe pin to it. "There! Now you can see this is most certainly giraffe fur."

I laughed and was satisfied. When The Peace March walked out of Griffith Park on the first day of March, out of Los Angeles on our initial 15-mile day, I hung the red cotton bag around my neck. It was with me all the way. On days too hot for man or dog, I staggered, clutched my totem bag, thought myself a giraffe and straightened. My legs stretched out. My eyes scanned the horizon. I undulated rhythmically along as sweat trickled down my back. A friend who had panted along behind me, caught up and said, "I watched you, Donna, and you suddenly became taller. You walked with grace and ease. How'd you do that?"

For over 3,700 miles, during 261 days, my quiet giraffe and I stuck our necks out for the common good.

Penny Harper and the Giraffe

Penny Harper was thin, almost gaunt. Her thick, glossy auburn hair swung about her prominent cheekbones, sometimes getting into her intensely direct, hazel eyes. She was almost 40, never married, a curious woman whose mother, Victoria, shrugged apologetically when referring to her daughter.

She said, "Penny lives in Los Angeles where she is president of a UFO group, for heaven's sakes! She has friends who talk about para-psychology, if you can imagine!"

I met Penny in Rhode Island. In Shelter Harbor, Rhode Island, when her sister Holly Harper was marrying my son, John Love, on May 24, 1986, in an 18th-century, stone church where the Harper girls had attended Episcopal Sunday School. Their family home was a grey shingle "cottage" surrounded by green sloping lawns, bright flowers and groves of deciduous trees. Admiral (retired) Talbot and Victoria Harper graciously entertained John's and Holly's relatives at an outdoor brunch. Down stone steps, on the dock at the edge of the salt pond, in the midst of the party, I found Penny sitting alone.

"Please join me," she invited. "Tell me about the Peace March you left for the weekend to come to the wedding. The group is in Denver, isn't it?" I summarized quickly because I wanted to talk about her proclaimed abilities as a medium. I had never met a medium.

She lost some of her reserve and, brushing her hair aside, eagerly explained the spirit who comes through her. "Want to have a session?" she proposed.

"Yes! Do you think anyone would mind? How about now?"

The library was at the end of the hall and quiet. I watched Penny draw the draperies, set a lighted candle on the floor, pull a multi-colored knitted afghan about herself. "Just sit comfortably on the sofa," she suggested, "and I'll sit here on the floor near the candle. My spirit person is a gentleman from India. You might be surprised at the high pitch of his voice."

I was surprised that I was even doing this! Especially surprised when I heard the bride's father Talbot and Jim Love, the groom's father, approaching along the hallway on a tour of the house. The library door opened a crack and Jim Love's head intruded halfway past the edge. "Oh, excuse me," was his startled response. He told me the next day, "That Penny is weird! Talbot was showing me the house and I looked into the library and there was Penny sitting on the floor, wrapped in a blanket, staring at a candle and chanting something foreign. Right in the middle of the party, too." The door had shielded me from his view.

Penny had been correct when explaining that her spirit's voice would be different from hers. Instead of the calm, cool melody of Penny's, I heard the high, singsong voice of India.

"Ah," he said. "I see above and behind you the doves of peace. They are hovering."

I commented to myself, "Of course they are hovering, I'm just taking a weekend off from the Great Peace March." This much Penny knew.

"And there are snakes of earth wisdom twining about your ankles," he continued. "That is very fortunate. Ah, I see you are going to St. Louis."

"No," I answered, "I have no plans to go to St. Louis and neither does the Peace March."

"But, you must. I see the Arch of St. Louis and you are beneath it. Wait! This is most unusual. It is not the Arch. It is a giraffe. You are sitting between the spraddled front legs of a giraffe who is curving her neck in an attempt to bring her face down close to yours. You are protected and guided by a giraffe."

"Amazing!" I leaned forward. "Penny, come back! Are you back yet?"

For a moment she was still. Then she opened her eyes, took a deep breath and spoke in her familiar voice. She sounded like clear water over smooth stones when she asked, "Tell me what happened. I think there was some confusion."

She didn't appear surprised as I related the story of Lynn Andrews' suggestion, "Get a totem."

"Yes," she smiled, "that seems right. I am happy this has meant something to you and that we have had this time together. Now, perhaps we should join the others?"

March Miracles

In interviews, members of the 1986 Great Peace March for Global Nuclear Disarmament were repeatedly asked the same question, "Why are you doing this walk?"

To break the monotony, Katea sometimes answered teasingly, "I'm walking for thin thighs."

Ted bragged, "Gonna camp in Central Park."

Leanne occasionally complained with a chuckle, "This is NOT the March I signed up for! Sometimes I wonder just why I'm here."

In the last half of May the Peace March had reached Denver. About 400 people had camped and walked since March 1, and were almost one-third of the way to Washington, DC. We had walked through the Mojave Desert, across Utah, over Loveland Pass in the Rockies, and were now having a rally on the steps of the Colorado State Capital Building. After rain, snow, sleet, and wind, and some scorchers, several of us relaxed on the lawns and stretched leg muscles in the spring sunshine. Leanne was first to notice a serious looking young woman draped in tape-recording gear. Followed by the ubiquitous TV cameraman, she was walking toward us. Another interview!

She introduced herself as a reporter for a local TV station and hunkered down among us. Sure enough, she asked each of us, "Why are you on the Great Peace March?" Since she seemed so serious, we gave her serious answers. I told her I was walking to create a more peaceful world for our grandchildren. Katea listed political reasons and Leanne told of her fears of nuclear bombs. Then the reporter lowered her mike. "I've heard of march miracles. Can you tell me about them?" We liked this question and encouraged the young woman to tape our answers.

"Yes!" Katea responded. "My favorite is one of the early ones. In the desert on a desolate power line road, we were trailing along out in nowhere with no one to see we were walking and suffering for Peace. It was hot, lonely, depressing. We had been out there five weeks. One day we began to talk about foods we craved.

David wanted watermelon, Dick craved orange juice. I would have traded my shoes for ice cream.

"We rounded an outcropping and there was a pickup truck. A man, a woman, and a girl stood next to it holding ice cream scoopers. Marchers lined up, cheered, cried, washed their hands and faces with canteen water, and sang. This family had driven from Los Angeles loaded with enough ice cream and cones for 400 weary walkers. They knew we were out there and had come to let us know we weren't forgotten. That is just one of many march miracles."

Katea had barely finished her story when Leanne leaned forward. "What about the gamblers in Vegas?" She took the mike and explained, "The March was stalled west of Las Vegas. We needed money to proceed. In the middle of the night, two lanky men in jeans and cowboy hats approached the campsite entrance and said to the gatekeepers, "We have something for the Peace Marchers. Will you get someone here to accept it?'

"Sleepy Marchers emerged from tents. One man told them he'd been lucky in gambling and wanted to share his winnings. He divided the money among those standing around him. Someone brought an empty, gallon-size mayonnaise jar and suggested that those who wished could put their gift in to share with the entire March. Next morning, those who counted the money, found $1,800. The number 18 is the same configuration as the Hebrew symbol for life. That man gave life to the March. That's a march miracle."

Leanne handed me the mike. "I have a small one," I began. "It was an especially hot day. We were camped in a parched stubble field behind a dam in western Colorado. Some walkers dashed up the embankment to go swimming. I wandered over toward the mail bus with Jonnie. She asked for a drink of water from my canteen. I held it out to her and said, "If only we had ice!" At that precise moment a truck wheeled in through the gate and headed toward us. The window was rolled down, an arm extended out, and swinging from the hand was a bag of ice! Without a word, the driver slowed down so we could grab the ice, and then headed toward the mobile kitchen. Jonnie and I ran ice up and down our faces, arms and legs and gave away the rest to others who were standing in the mail line."

"Want another one?" Ted offered.

"I think I've got it," the reporter retrieved her mike and pocketed it.

The cameraman coiled his lines, stood a moment gazing at us, and then blurted, "You guys are the greatest!"

The reporter extended her hand, smiled, and thanked us. Suddenly, she lost her professionalism, clutched Leanne in a hug, and cried, "I wish I could go with you! I need a miracle!"

Gene Gordon and The Great Peace March

I got an email from Gene Gordon this week. (In August 2004) He was on the Peace March. He was the very first Marcher I met... well, that is, after Connie, the woman who, in May of 1985, had told me "about the walk I'm going to take next year." She said the Great Peace March was to start March 1, 1986, in Los Angeles and end in Washington, DC November 15. I knew I would go, too, although I didn't know quite how. I was 58 years old, director of a tutorial services center, had community responsibilities. It took major planning, matched by personal commitment.

I met Gene a month before the great Peace March began when he organized several San Francisco Bay Area people to walk in protest in San Jose on a winter Sunday afternoon. About a dozen of us trailed along at the edges of streets. We carried hand printed placards and raised our hands in the peace sign. I was so embarrassed to be calling attention to myself. Drivers shouted, honked their horns, gave us a friendly wave or the finger. Thank goodness only a few people were downtown that day.

Gene was an experienced activist. He was politically informed, had a career in radio, was a writer, a performer. He'd been at it for more than 20 years. I was a conservative San Francisco Peninsula housewife. True, I had been divorced for 15 years, but nevertheless, I lived life not greatly different from when I was married and a busy mother. Gene's idea of getting some of us together was a good one. For me it was a gentle introduction to what was going to happen on March 1, when 1,200 people were to gather in Los Angeles and begin a 3,700-mile walk.

On that day the sidewalks along our route were lined with crowds of enthusiastic supporters. We carried balloons and professionally printed placards. We chanted. The mayor spoke. Holly Near sang. We were celebrities capturing the imagination of people whose lives didn't allow them to leave on a long walk across America. For peace. The Great Peace March for Global Nuclear Disarmament.

Once the March actually began, I didn't see a lot of Gene. We walked together enough for me to hear him say he once lived at

Stanford. I immediately assumed he's been a student there. But, no, he had lived in a tent or a camper far up in the hills, had used the school facilities, and launched his career as a radio commentator. I had never met anyone who chose to live like that.

He walked on most days, rain or shine, pleasant or stormy, with Rhoda, a carpenter from Seattle, and as they walked along together, they read Shakespeare to each other. On rainy days they protected their books with Baggies. On windy days, by clutching them tightly. On rest days, they found a tree and read beneath it. Others were reading Shakespeare, too. Gene and Rhoda lead a performance of "Twelfth Night" when we camped at Lake Anita, Iowa. We camped in a county park where a floating swimming dock doubled as the stage. That was the first of three plays Gene and his friends produced during the nine months we walked from Los Angeles to Washington, DC.

I don't recall the third, but the second play was "Midsummer's Night's Dream" in Kearny, Nebraska on June 19. I remember Gene saying that he and Rhoda walked 20 miles "through a furnace" that Nebraska summer day. They worked all the day walking and forging the play. They took Shakespeare's "Dream", condensed it wholesale, related it entirely to the March. In every scene, with every character, we marchers saw ourselves reflected on stage. Every allusion and joke referred to life on the Great Peace March. In camp after a supper of stew and muffins, they rehearsed. Even in the chaos of camp, in the heat and exhaustion, every member of their cast showed up. The children of the March were the fairies in the play. The final performance for an audience sunburned and melted, was just what we needed. I loved the energy Gene and his cast still had after walking 15 to 20 hot miles a day.

Gene and Rhoda read all 37 of Shakespeare's plays. That's about one for every 100 miles of the March.

By the time we were in Washington, DC, 15,000 people walked in with us. The campsite was huge, sprawled, and impossible! The members of the core group of 400 who had walked the entire way lost track of each other. Some of us just checked into a hotel to maintain sanity. We sat on the floor, ate pizza, drank wine and fell into real beds. During those last days, Gene and I said goodbye to each other and never again were in touch.

After 18 years, I am glad to hear from him. Gene says he lives in Walnut Creek's Rossmoor Village on Golden Rain Road, Entry 3, Number 12. He continues to write for publication as well as corresponding with Peace Marchers. One, Shabtai, wrote to Gene recently to say there was a news article in the Santa Cruz Sentinel mentioning the Peace March. Gene looked it up and found it was about a group of women, The CRONES COUNSEL, who met at my house to see the one-hour Great Peace March video "One Step At a Time." The article concluded, "After watching the film the women agreed to walk in The Human Race in Santa Cruz on Saturday, May 8." The Crones will have collected funds to be contributed to a Peace cause.

I'll tell Gene about the May 8 walk when I see him in Carpinteria, CA in September at a Great Peace March Reunion.

The Eighteenth Great Peace March Reunion

Last weekend, September 24-26, 2004, I drove down Highway 101 to Carpinteria to attend the 18th reunion of the Great Peace March for Global Nuclear Disarmament. It's been 18 years since more than 400 of us walked from Los Angeles to Washington, DC. Over 14 years since I lived in the Santa Barbara area and drove back and forth to San Mateo to check on my house and visit my families. The hills around San Luis Obispo are still golden, studded by dark oak trees. The deli next to the gas station at the Shell Beach exit still makes delicious turkey sandwiches. Carpinteria is now a busy beach community. So many memories. Returning was like stepping through a rusty gate to those transitional days after the March and before I married Mike. Now that Mike and I are no longer married, I was free to attend a Peace March Reunion.

I didn't set up a tent at the campground in the State Park at the end of Palm Avenue. I checked into Motel 6, room 246. Right next door, in 247, were Ann and Dick Edelman! We three had become friends on the March and they were a main reason for my attending this, my first, reunion. Before going over to the campground, we agreed with Dick's suggestion, "let's just hang out in the motel room and have a visit." Like old times, that spontaneity.

At the campground, familiar faces beamed at me. Some admired my old red sweatshirt I had had printed with Great Peace March on the front and across the back, my father's response upon hearing the plan:

GoddamnestdummestthingIeverheardof.

I unfolded my new yellow camp chair and plopped down next to Mim, as she sat fiddling with her cane. Mim, at 86, was the eldest at the reunion. Still full of sparks and intensity, she talked about falling in love with Sam from Cleveland and tenting with him "off to the side where I wouldn't feel so conspicuous." We recalled a day almost exactly 18 years ago in Pennsylvania when we wakened to red maple leaves littering the campground and silver frost rimming the seams of our gumdrop tents. "Well," Mim sighed, "That was a day long ago. Sam still lives with his wife in Cleveland and I still live in

Los Angeles, so ours is a romance of emails in which we proclaim our love for each other." She jabbed the dust with her cane.

Coleen, a major organizer during the March, sat now by the campfire and held on her lap, a two-year-old grandniece, whose mother is on drugs so Coleen has the baby living with her. Someone told me that even though Coleen and her husband are in their 50's, they hope to legally adopt the child.

Gene Gordon, wiry to almost gaunt, wandered over to where I was sitting. Gene and I had met before the March and hadn't seen each other since. I gave him a hug and an essay I'd written about his reading all of Shakespeare while walking across America. He was delighted and went off to show it to his wife, June. Next morning, they gravely presented me with their recent book, Tales of Wo-Chi-Ca, (Workers Children's Camp) about June's childhood experiences in a New Jersey summer camp during Depression years. There, Blacks, Asians, Puerto Ricans and Italians learned to live happily together. Gene and June continue to write for radical publications.

Bob brought with him his adopted daughter, a lovely, young, dark skinned Ethiopian girl. He showed us plot plans of the 90 acres in Belize he is developing. He plans a school for local children, a health center and parcels for homes. He invited us all down for a visit. Someone replied, "If the draft goes through, we'll move down there!"

Sue bounced over to greet me and we drew our chairs close together. I remembered her summary of the March's arrival in Washington, DC. "This certainly is a 14-hanky day, isn't it." as we hugged each other for the last time. Now we hugged each other again and she talked about her husband Roy. They live in Morgan Hill near a creek where an old wooden public bridge had deteriorated. "Roy tore it down and was building a new bridge when the city inspector came by to ask if he had a permit. He didn't, of course, so was red-tagged. But," Sue continued, "A city engineer came out and after looking over the project, removed the red tag, shook Roy's hand and thanked him for building a stronger, better bridge. And, imagine! Roy didn't even do the whole March!"

Bea, who lives in Carpinteria, showed me one of the several trees she has had planted in public places. One for each Peace

Marcher who has died. She also drove Mim and me as well as Jolene to lunch and around to see places I loved when I lived there right after the March. We prayed in silence in the Vendanta Temple, visited Casa Maria where I'd attended workshops and where now Jolene has a garden in memory of her son, her only child, Kirk, killed in a windsurfing accident several years ago. Jolene is furious with the world. She was furious on the March, too. She writes books to tell her story, to vent her anger and, she says, "to promote Peace, of course."

On and on, one story of commitment after another! I was stunned by the simple, plainly stated reports of lives over the past 18 years. Before I'd arrived, I had determined to speak to those I'd known on the March in one-on-one conversations because I'd thought the reunion would be like a cocktail party. Light, superficial comments interrupted by others who drifted by. I was wrong. The conversations were sincere, caring, full of attentive listening and honest exchanges of concerns and joys. I found myself moved almost to tears by the magnificence of these casually dressed people idling in a dusty campground.

Even dressed casually, Katea is a striking woman with an admirable sense of style. The daughter of wealthy parents in Palo Alto where she attended Castilejo School for Girls, she joined the March in outright rebellion against all that her conservative parents represented and changed her name from Katherine. In Colorado, looking for a shower, Katea met a motel manager, Brian, and, as she says, "I seduced him. He let me have a shower and then he quit his job and joined the March." They are married, live in the hills behind Santa Barbara and have two children: Ruben who at 17 is having school trouble and Emily Rose, a sweet mentally retarded 12-year-old. Katea is suing the school district for not serving the academic needs of their children. She has cashed in a million dollar inheritance to pay a lawyer $800,000 in a landmark case demanding that schools educate all children.

Sunday morning 30 or so of us Great Peace March graduates stood in a circle, holding hands, singing March songs, which Ann and Katea led. Katea swayed over to Carlos de la Fuente, a 66-year-old retired attorney, and asked him to step into the center of the circle so we could sing to him our blessings. He will paddle his kayak from Santa Barbara to Costa Rica, a 2,500-mile journey that will take six months.

He wants to call attention to his concerns about environmental destruction. He says, "It breaks my heart, what is happening to the Baja Peninsula, to our oceans. The pollution, the degradation. We are leaving our children a terrible legacy." Carlos came to each one of us in the circle to exchange hugs. I told him this is the 18th year since the March and in Hebrew the symbol that looks like 18 means new life. A reminder that he'll infuse new life into our planet.

I looked around the circle at our diverse group. Interracial, international, intergenerational, intercultural. Next to me, holding my hand, stood a woman I hadn't yet seen at the reunion. She and her two small daughters were on the March. I remember Mariana as having perfect glowing skin and a bright smile. She and Carlos met on the March and have been married for 17 years. She still glows. I said to her, "I guess what we all have in common is that no one here thinks inside the box."

She paused in thought, then grinned, "What box?"

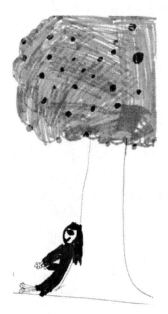

Pay Back

In the early 1980's I was living in San Mateo, not far from the San Francisco airport. One day my brother John called from Eugene, Oregon. "Hi, have any spare time next week?" He explained that Akima was flying back to Japan soon. She wanted to see San Francisco and John asked if I could act as hostess and tour guide for her. I could.

John, his wife Gayle, and their four children lived in a spacious old square house not far from the University of Oregon campus. For several years they hosted a series of Japanese students. Akima was one who had lived with them and recently had graduated. I met her at the San Francisco airport and took her home with me.

We both enjoyed our days of exploring sights, Stanford University, Sawyer Camp Walking Trail, Half Moon Bay, the Coyote Point Museum of Natural History. Eventually I returned her to the airport. On our way, she opened her purse and said, "I want to pay you for what you have done for me." Her delicate hands fumbled with money.

She looked past her drape of black straight hair at me when I replied, "No, Akima, you may not pay me." I was a bit miffed but chalked it up to cultural differences. "On second thought," I added, "there is a way you can pay me. Someday, when you can, you share your hometown with a visiting stranger. In this way, you can contribute to international understanding and perhaps to world peace." She closed her purse and smiled.

About five years later, after brother John had attended her wedding in Kyoto and had received a baby announcement, I got a post card from Akima. It said, "Dear Mrs. Love, Today I paid you back."

That was all. That was enough.

Good Morning!

May 10, 1999, was a bright Monday morning in Southwestern Oregon's Umpqua River Valley. Along the road that meandered above the river, I drove toward the chiropractor's office in Yoncalla. Behind his office he had two rooms crowded with exercise equipment. A workout gym right there in a brick building that 100 years ago was the Beckley Brothers Dry Goods Store. As I entered the backdoor, my friend Lucille Gehling waved from a treadmill. She wiped perspiration from her bright face and chirped, "How was your winter? Haven't seen you since last Fall! Do you miss Capitola? Are you glad to be back? "

My husband Mike and I divided our time between winters in Capitola with a population of 10,000 and summers in the country outside Elkton, the second smallest incorporated town in Oregon, population 147. We were mostly alone together, working on Shaws' Corner. Mike mowed one and a half acres of lawn, his afternoon beer perched on the seat beside him. We discussed what to have for dinner, how to get rid of the moles, what to watch on TV. Adjacent to the new garden-in-the-round, an inviting potting shed stood beneath masses of pink Luther roses. I devoted time to digging and planting, harvesting and canning. Our place had 17 feet of alluvial topsoil. Bob Down-the-Road told us it is the best soil in Douglas County. I became a revered gardener even though a novice. Everything grew! I felt close to Mother Earth there and weeded through long, still summer evenings. For hours I knelt in the silence of the garden to pull weeds and crumble the soil, to sit back on my heels and survey my world.

The next morning I'd be up early, click on the coffee, pull on a warm jacket and rubber shoes to emerge into another day. Greeted by swallows, crows, ospreys, and robins, I paused at the arched garden entrance to watch and listen. The sheep stampeded to the near edge of the pasture and peered through the fence. The braver ones snuffled about for a handout, maybe a bucket of apple cores if I'd made applesauce. In the damp mornings, they stank like old wet wool socks.

In contrast, the Capitola home was a 1,000 square foot, one bedroom, one bath, nuthin' yard, picket-fence cottage. We were in the midst of five sons and their families, Mike's brother and sister, and friends we've had for fifty years. There were groups for walking, a Crone Counsel, classes for bridge, computer, yoga, religious history, art, and writing as well as Alanon and CoDA. We had neighbors who congregated in the street to chat.

During winter months in Capitola, I have taken morning coffee out by the benches on the cliff to watch the sun rise over Aptos beyond Monterey Bay. I have felt connected to all Creation, related to the vast rhythms of moon, water, and tides. I have listened to roaring storms measured by foam crashing beneath, and sometimes onto, the wharf. One morning I was so excited to get out to the benches, I grabbed camera and tea and hurried out the door. I forgot to close it and forgot I was still in my sleeping sweats. Oh, well. No one would be up so early. I hurried to catch the light as it changed from rose to apricot to pearl to pure. I stood transfixed, forgot to take pictures, and let the tea get cold. I hardly noticed a car door as it closed behind me. Then I heard Katie-Down-the-Street chuckling. I turned toward her. There she was, camera in hand. She wore a green velour bathrobe over her white cotton nighty. "Never mind," she said. "This is Santa Cruz County. Sleeping attire is acceptable."

The early mornings in Capitola and in Elkton reminded me of Alamos in Mexico, where I had a little house for a while. There I got out of bed at dawn to walk along cobbled streets whose sunny walls were draped with brilliant bougainvillea. I heard the murmurings of Mexican women as they fingered their rosaries in morning services. Their voices blended with those of doves in the towers.

Even now, after fifteen years, I have longed for the beach at Condo Pilar near San Carlos in Sonora. I rented there for about six weeks before I found the house in Alamos. A friend showed me a cool tiled studio apartment whose sliding glass doors opened onto a strip of rough grass and a row of palm trees, the beach beyond. I wove baskets. I ate breakfast, lunch and then dinner out on the sand. Watched sparkles on the water. Watched the sun go down beyond the rusty swing set stranded in the surf where pelicans roosted.

Some days I walked down the beach beyond the small sand hills to the estero and silently watched birds. I made mini-shrines of found objects, bleached shells and tiny twigs that littered the shore. When I unfolded and lay on the warm sand, I listened to small rustlings and soft bird calls in the willows.

I think of those days with great tenderness. Mostly I was alone, but one day sitting in a circle of acquaintances doing yoga on the grass, a woman I didn't recognize asked, "Aren't you Donna Love? Didn't we meet in Abijan?" Yes! She and I were two of nine people who spent a few weeks in 1985 in Western Africa studying traditional healing. She lived in Minnesota and here she was on a beach in Mexico! Both of us out of context. Aah, Mexican magic.

In Oregon, I listened to the homing pigeons in the barn next door, and imagined I could hear the doves in high towers of Alamos. I imagined I stood in the church's long shadow as it fell across the grimy benches and gardens in the plaza. I heard the scratching of the brush brooms as wrinkled old people swept the eternal dust into homemade dustpans. I smelled the smoke of early-day fires. Sometimes a cow ambled along the street with an empty beer can tied to her tail. The can rattled on the cobbles so the owner could find her when he woke up.

⚜

Five years have passed since Lucille greeted me in the workout gym behind the chiropractor's office in Yoncalla. I no longer stand at the garden gate in rural Oregon to watch ospreys high up or listen to the homing pigeons next door. Mike and I are no longer married. He still lives in rural Oregon. I live in Capitola. Alone. Alone except for my sons and their families, friends I've known for 50 years or five months, and groups for any interest I wish to pursue.

I have walked along the sand in Capitola at the end of a winter's day, recalled similar strolls in Mexico, and have come to know that the numinous times for me are those in which I am alone. The places I have yearned for are those in which I have been alone enough to grow my soul.

Rush to the Rescue

I felt like shouting, "We did it, everybody! We did it!"

Every May the barn swallows wanted to build their nests under the eaves at the gable end of Mike's and my farmhouse near Elkton in Southwestern Oregon. They swarmed, clouds of them. In even numbers, of course. They swooped and dodged, lodged up high above the bathroom window. Pairs nestled in, looking smug and permanent. They flowed out again when I stood down on the little deck and waved a bath towel and shouted.

Mike followed Bob-Down-the-Road's advice and aimed the garden hose to squirt the first mud daubs away, only to check an hour later to find more birds that liked our house and were making a mess. Margie-in-Town told Mike, "Get your orchard ladder and climb up to squirt Raid. Them birds don't like Raid." Mike was up and down the ladder for most of the day. Finally the sun set and the birds went off somewhere.

Next morning before we were up, they were back. I got a Ram Dass lecture tape, one with sudden bursts of laughter and applause, plugged in the tape player, set it out on the deck and draped it with a protective towel. I turned up the volume. The birds went away. We turned over the tape every 40 minutes. If we let it lapse, the swallows reappeared.

I decided they wouldn't notice that our radio reception in the country wasn't very clear and tuned in Rush Limbaugh, turned him up and redraped the towel. Mike and I got ready to go into Eugene. As I dressed, I watched out the window. The birds came by, listened, hovered for a tentative moment, shuddered, and left.

Later in the day, the neighbors next door happily announced that wonderful large numbers of swallows were building nests up under the eaves of their old barn.

When I told a friend, she cheered, "You did it!" She chuckled, "Just proves that even bird-brains don't like Rush Limbaugh."

Picking Blackberries

In the summer of 1999, I parked above Yellow Creek in rural Douglas County in southwest Oregon, about 15 miles from Mike's and my place in the country, to go pick blackberries. I hacked my way into the brambles and balanced on downed branches. I stretched up toward the highest clusters, avoided the thorns, popped the prime center berries onto my tongue, stained my fingers, and talked to myself about making jam. Surrounded by silence except for the bees, I remembered other briar patch days. Back to early childhood, to young motherhood, and to a time full of desperate loneliness. As I picked, I dreamed and drifted.

The berries oozed juice of such fragrance that I was carried back into my Grandmother Taylor's kitchen over 70 years ago when I watched her making jam. She wore a cotton apron pinned at the bib corners to her dress. Her stout amplitude protected, she hefted pots around on the stove. The kitchen was large and yellow, with a row of windows open to the backyard where steam escaped. A canary sat in his cage on a stand near the built-in sideboard. Grandmother let me carry the cage by the ring at the top. I loved that bird! His song mixed with the promise of toast and warm jam.

As I found another thicket above Yellow Creek, the sun, warm on my back, felt just as it did when I was almost seven and my brother John was five. It was a day in the summer of 1934 when Mother gave us small pails to carry as we trooped from our house across Fourth Street in Coquille to get her friend Mrs. Rosae. We all walked what seemed a long way, probably two lengthy blocks, to the near end of the Fourth Street Bridge and down the slope. Jungles of blackberry vines supported gobs of bursting berries. John and I picked and ate while Mother and Mrs. Rosae, in their broad straw hats, picked and talked. When the sun made us sleepy, John and I polished off the rest of our berries and sat on our upended buckets. "When can we go home?" he sighed. His blond hair glistened, his nose was getting pink.

Eventually we straggled back and waved goodbye to Mrs. Rosae. In the kitchen, Mother hung up her hat and took the green-handled metal potato masher from the drawer. She smashed some berries, stirred in white sugar and spread butter onto thick slices of home-baked bread. On top, she spooned the dark gooey purpley berry mix. John and I took our snack out to sit on the back porch steps. We didn't speak. We ate.

A generation later in Augusts when my sons were in grammar school, I drove them from our home in Hillsborough, California, up to visit Mother and Pop at their old yellow vacation house on Ten-Mile Lake in Southwestern Oregon. In early mornings Mother knotted shoelaces through holes punched in the tops of empty quart milk cartons and hung one around each boy's neck. "Now," she shooed them outside, "come back when your cartons are full." When they returned, Pop made them pancakes, which Mother slathered with butter, crushed berries and white sugar.

After the boys had grown and their father and I were divorced, I continued to live for a while in Hillsborough. One empty day I walked the two miles to downtown and noticed a few blackberry bushes hovering on the back border of the San Mateo Medical Clinic parking lot on Baldwin Avenue. I stopped, filled a styrofoam coffee cup, and breathed the dark warm aroma. The berries were dusty and not very juicy, but wandering home, eating them one by one, I felt better.

In recent years, I've heard my son John, now in his forties, explain to his daughter Sarah, "We grew up in a blackberry culture. Here's a milk carton for you. Come on, let's go. I saw a berry patch up the road."

Each August during the 1990's when I once again lived in Oregon, my son Matt drove his family from Morgan Hill, California, "The berries are ripe, aren't they, Mom?" His birthday is in August and his chosen celebration dessert is still blackberry dumplings. Ever since boyhood summers at Ten-Mile Lake, he has called it Country Pudding. Mother started it. She layered a baking pan with fresh blackberries dotted with spoons of butter, sprinkled with sugar and cinnamon, covered with Bisquick dumplings, and baked it to brown and bubbling.

Yes, we in the Blackberry Culture await the ripening season. Each summer I pick gallons and make jam. Dozens of jars to give at Christmastime. Jams that smell like my Grandmother Taylor's kitchen.

Memories connect when I'm picking blackberries. I'm filled with thoughts of sun-warmed, fragrant, bee-buzzing summer days. With me are all the gatherers who have gone before us; cave-dweller women, Native American women, our grandmother's grandmothers, our own mothers. To follow are those who will be wearing quart milk cartons around their necks and may be lucky enough to have Country Pudding.

What's a Fence?

Several years ago I decided to upgrade the fences around the country place where my husband and I lived. New fences to keep the sheep in and deer out, a white fence along the driveway to delineate the edge between grass and gravel, a rustic rail fence around the garden for roses to climb. Also, new gates in these new fences.

One day, I opened a gate, walked through, turned to latch it again, and asked myself, what's with this obsession about new fences and gates? After all, what are they? Enclosures, divisions, barriers, confines, boundaries. BOUNDARIES! Wahoo! I was practicing building boundaries!

I began practicing in more personal ways. With words, gestures, facial expressions. Enough! I finally said. Enough rudeness. Enough verbal abuse. I practiced detachment. Spent more time away from Mike. Breathed bigger, laughed with friends, treated myself well. Made castle walls with peepholes, ramparts from which to view the terrain, enough geographical distance so I didn't hear the roaring. I attended Alanon meetings, found a sponsor; found a psychologist, a chiropractor, a massage therapist. The only changes were the ones I made.

Ultimately, that raging lovable husband and I divorced. A definitive boundary. If only living together had been healthy for each of us! The final gate has opened and shut behind me. I would not have had the courage to make these changes without professional and Alanon support.

Now in Capitola, I stand on the cliffs above Monterey Bay and gaze at the fenceless, boundless landscape extending to the far horizon. I raise my arms in gratitude.

Dawning of a Friendship

One very early morning in the Fall of maybe 1997, I stepped out onto the front porch to peek at the eastern sky. It took away my breath. So totally brilliant with all my favorite colors. Red! Orange! Peach! Apricot! Pearl! I dashed back inside to grab the camera and my cup of tea, neglected to shut the door, and raced out to the benches above the cliff to stand transfixed. I forgot to take pictures. The tea grew cold. I was close to tears at the beauty of this place where I live when suddenly I realized I was outside, in public, in my pajamas!

Even before I could glance around to see if anyone else was up and on the street, I heard a car pull up. The door opened and shut. I heard a chuckle and turned to see a tousled woman in a green velour bathrobe with her camera in hand. She saw my embarrassment and laughed, "It's all right. This is Santa Cruz. Nobody cares."

Thus I met Katie-Down-the-Street.

Note: I know I'm repeating a story told on page 71, but that's the way we grandmothers are! Sometimes we repeat.

More Watermelon, Please

Mother was 97. On the coast of Oregon, in Florence, she lived in her own home, albeit with help from professional caregivers, family, and neighbors. Her greatest fear had been intruders, a man in the middle of the night invading her home. But now she lived in a gated community and felt safe. Her new greatest fear was falling and breaking her hip.

One Sunday she was home alone having enjoyed cubes of watermelon the caregiver had left for her. Mother got up and used her walker to navigate across the room to the refrigerator. She opened the door and used it to steady herself, reached in for more watermelon, got it. The door moved. She fell. Watermelon splattered everywhere! She lay on the kitchen floor pressing the button on her Medi-Mate until someone at the hospital figured out it might be Mother and phoned the neighbors next door. They had their own physical problems so phoned the neighbors across the street. Hal and Linda Lock came to lift her and couldn't. They called the paramedics. One of the rescuers was a friend of Mother's local grandson, Dan, so called him. Dan called me at the farm, an hour away, to say, "Aunt Donna, Grandmother has fallen and they're taking her to the hospital. Mom and Dad are out of town somewhere, I don't know where. My wife Vicki is out of town and Riley is in the bathtub. What shall I do?"

Poor Dan, in his mid-thirties, he has had his share of "the duty." Eighteen months ago, while Mike and I were away in Capitola for the winter and Dan's parents were still circumnavigating, Dan called to say, "Donna, Uncle John has died while he was on a business trip in Ho Chi Min City. My parents are out of town and who should tell Grandmother?"

He did. He drove over, sat at her feet, held her hand, looked her in the eye, and said, "Grandmother, I don't know how to tell you this." She replied, "It's all right, Dan. Just tell me." John was her eldest son, named for her father, John William. It was a terrible loss.

And now Dan had asked me, "What shall I do?" I could hear him sigh. "I guess I'll get Riley out of the tub and we'll go over to the hospital to see what's going on." Later he called again, "They've taken x-rays. She has fractured her hip. The caregiver is there and will do what is necessary. Grandmother will stay over night at the hospital."

What Mother had feared most had happened. Because of watermelon.

Her best old family stories were about watermelon. Almost every spring during our growing-up years, she told us about her brother Glenn who gave up watermelon for Lent. In Glenn's day, watermelons became available July 4th. Another favorite was about her Uncle Herm, who at family reunion picnics in Albany in the early 1900's, ate the best part out of the center slice of watermelon and put the circle of rind around his neck. Then he ate the end piece and popped the round rind onto his head. Juice trickled down as he danced to entertain the children. He raced everyone down to the shallow edge of the Willamette River to dunk and wash and splash.

Now our family had another watermelon story: The Sunday that Grandmother Rankin got up to get some more and fell. When I visited her in the hospital on Monday, I asked her what she'd like me to bring her from home. "Well," she thought only a moment, "I'd still like some of that delicious watermelon."

One Last Boat in the Bay

There's only one boat left tied to a buoy in the waters off Capitola Wharf. During the summer I counted about 30. They reminded me of beach birds as they swung around all facing the same direction, up-wind, ruffled and bobbing through sunny days. All are gone now, except one, a sign of the changing seasons.

Early this morning, as I stood at the benches on Opal Cliffs above the railroad tracks, I watched that one remaining boat. It looked lonely. Feeling useless? Maybe like Mother felt before she, at one-hundred-and-a-half years, finally died about noon on November 8, 2002.

She died as she had lived, privately and with dignity. That week in a care center in Florence on the Oregon Coast where she had chosen to spend her last few years, she lay in bed and breathed with the help of oxygen. Her nearest grandson, Dan, held her hand, grinned when she winked at him, sat with her until she dozed off. On Friday he went home to call his parents, his Uncle Richard, and me, to say he thought the end was near. When he returned an hour later, she had died. When I called at the care center to talk with him, he told me, and I asked what he was doing. "I'm just sitting here waiting and having a beer with Grandmother."

Mother outlasted all her women friends in the small southwestern Oregon town of Coquille, where she and our father spent most of their adult lives, all her Garden Club friends, her art class and bridge buddies, her Republican Committee members. Camella Reitman, the dentist's wife, died the spring Mother celebrated her 100th birthday, but that didn't mean anything to Mother. She never did like Camella very much.

She was the last of her birth family, the last one born, the last to die. Her Cousin Isabella in Portland, who at 104 still reads library books and writes her own personal correspondence, says she misses their telephone conversations. Mother outlived our father by 17 years and our brother John by four. All five of her siblings, our Uncles Glenn, Ray, Ralph, Harry and Auntie Vera left several years ahead of her. So there she was, the last.

It was good she had about 60 members in her immediate family, most of whom gathered for her milestones and listened to her stories. Every time I asked her, "tell us the story about your favorite uncle," she'd smile and say, "Yes. He was my mother's, your Grandmother Taylor's, youngest brother, the one who got put in the pokey for embezzling money from the piano store. He loved us children!' At the end of her story Mother concluded, "He was our favorite uncle. Rather like your Uncle Glenn."

Our Uncle Glenn was Mother's eldest brother. He was fire chief in Roseburg, not very far from Coquille. A bachelor until his late 40's, he'd come over to go fishing with our father or maybe just stop by on his way somewhere up the coast. My three brothers and I, playing kick-the-can in the middle of Coulter Street with neighborhood kids, paused if we heard a siren. "Uncle Glenn! Here comes Uncle Glenn!" as he drove his bright red chief's car around the corner toward us. We'd stop playing, race for his whoops, hollers and hugs, follow him into the house, watch him grab our mother and see her love for him. Next, over to the pantry in the corner of kitchen, he opened the door and reached up for the Jim Beam. The bottle in one hand, he got a shot glass out of another cupboard, stood at the sink, poured, set the bottle aside, screwed on the lid, winked at us, lifted his tiny glass, threw his head back and expelled a sound of great satisfaction. He and Mother talked. We four listened and waited. Not for long. Uncle Glenn suddenly turned, roared and grabbed the nearest boy and wrestled him onto the braided rug in front of the fireplace. We'd all pile on, tumble and giggle, Uncle Glenn the biggest kid of all. Then his visit was over. Out the door, into his red car, one more wave, slam the car door, rev up the siren, and he'd be gone.

Mother didn't know until after Glenn's death, when she and our father were taking care of his estate, that Glenn was a half-brother. In a note from him, they read that his father had wanted to run off when he found his wife was pregnant. He agreed to stay until after the baby was born, then he disappeared. Glenn was about two when his mother married John William Taylor.

We hardly knew Mother's other brothers. She didn't like Ralph after she had helped finance him through medical school "and he turned out to be nothing but a God-damned drunk." She wouldn't be in the same room with Ray's wife who would "shriek like the proverbial fishwife." Harry and Pearl lived too far away, in Oakland, California. We knew Auntie Vera in Portland, but not well. Mother and Auntie Vera enjoyed window-shopping for dishes and diamonds, but we children didn't visit her often.

She didn't enjoy her own mother, our Grandmother Taylor, saying she had a violent temper and narrow mind. I do recall one visit, Thanksgiving of 1946, when Uncle Glenn came and so did Grandmother Taylor. She abhorred alcohol and said so. Our father and Uncle Glenn enjoyed a cocktail before dinner, but had to avoid Grandmother Taylor's glare. They hid their glasses in the back corners of the record player when she came into the living room. "Quick! Here she comes! Close the lid!" She wondered why my brothers and I crashed over with giggles.

Mother intensely disliked her mother-in-law, our Grandmother Sarah Dallas, mainly for "all the whining and asking for money." Sometimes Grandmother Dallas spoke of family history, of some well-known New England relatives. Mother sneered, the corner of her lip lifted, her nose twitched, "I don't believe in resting on one's laurels."

Pop's brother Charles was married to Eve, whom Mother thought snobbish. When our mother and father stopped by to visit them in Seattle, Eve invited them into the kitchen, bypassing the all-white living room and commenting they "save that room for important people." Uncle Jerry, Pop's older brother, and his wife Anna were kind and gentle, "good Christians." Mother tolerated them, but didn't like their children, Robert and Ruth.

So Mother looked to her own children, and to theirs, for family warmth. She was a dutiful wife, a responsible mother, loving and generous to her 14 grandchildren, 29 great-grandchildren and one great-great grandson. Her humor and discipline were her strengths. She was a feisty woman, bright and spirited. Sometimes she felt trapped by the smallness of Coquille, the endless needs of four children, the high profile of being a doctor's wife. She shuddered when someone called her, "Mrs. Dr. Rankin." I think one of her great enthusiasms, besides playing the piano, was color. In her knitting, painting, gardening, flower arranging, interior design, and wardrobe, color dominated her choices.

It was no great surprise that as I headed from Capitola to Florence the day after her death, I drove right through the end of a rainbow. Above the rain-wet I-5 near Weed, in Northern California, my friend Katie-Down-the-Street and I noted a rainbow in the eastern hills. It arched up and over, shining onto the roadbed, on the hood of the car, right through the windshield and onto my hands as they gripped the steering wheel. We both gasped. Then I explained, "That was Mother saying goodbye. She's sprung free and is going on."

I Hear You, Mother!

Mother was smart, resourceful, inventive as well as opinionated and outspoken. She took her roles of housewife and mother seriously and taught her children by example and edict. These are some of her statements:

Walk with dignity and no one will notice (the run in your stocking or that your slip is showing). I've used this when entering a room of strangers and wondering if I'm properly dressed. It works.

Be modest in dress and behavior.

Have your own tools. Every housewife must have her own so she'll know where they are when she needs them. Mother's tack hammer, claw hammer, screwdrivers and pliers, along with small boxes of nails and screws, and a coil of picture wire were kept in a cloth bag in a bottom drawer in the kitchen.

Take care of possessions. Keep the mixer, can-opener, the kitchen scale clean. Hang up your clothes in the closet. Wipe the clothesline clean before hanging the laundry. Keep the refrigerator clean and orderly. I remember her opening the Frigidaire door, drawing up a chair, and, bathed in the light of the interior globe, she took out the containers, wiped them clean, wiped the shelves, threw out the moldy leftovers, and said, with finality, "There!" as she shut the door. What about the car? She took such care of her dark blue Mercedes-Benz (the first one in Coquille), that she wouldn't let me learn to drive. I got my license in Eugene after I married at age 21.

Put a little sugar in the boiling water when cooking corn. The corn needs only six minutes and will be sweeter. If you've just picked the corn after you put the water on to boil, you don't need the sugar.

Crumble eggshells into a glass of water and let it sit overnight. Strain water onto plants. Pour leftover tea onto ferns and other acid-loving plants. Empty coffee grounds into flowerbeds.

Only cheap girls wear red shoes. I was probably 50 before I bought red shoes, and then never felt comfortable in them. I gave them to Goodwill.

Marry a man with clean fingernails. I think she meant marry a man who works primarily with his head, rather than his hands.

Don't rest on your laurels. Keep accumulating them.

In Portland, stay at the Mallory Hotel. "It's a lovely old building and Pop likes the breakfast there. The Benson is nice, but people from Eastern Oregon stay there. We from southwestern Oregon stay at the Mallory."

Don't hang out downtown with your friends. Come home and help with the ironing.

Polish the silver, set the table with care. Be sure the napkins are folded neatly. After all, you've just ironed them.

Save recipes. You'll find them on tin-can labels and food boxes, in magazines, William Sonoma catalogues, and newspapers. Save them all and someday perhaps even use one. I did tear out and save recipes the first four months of Jim's and my marriage and I used them until Christmas when I received The Joy of Cooking from my brothers. I still use it 55 years later. I still tear out recipes, too.

Don't write anything you'd be embarrassed to see in the newspaper. Would she approve of our current recommendations to journal? I wonder if she'd have had less trouble with her "tender tummy" if she'd written her frustrations.

She recommended, "When angry, make yeast bread." She made lots of bread. All fine grained and evenly textured, which she accomplished by raising the handful of dough over her head to slam it into the corner of the kitchen counter. In a 4-H Bread Baking Contest, I got only second prize. Guess I wasn't angry enough.

Take a walk around the block after dinner. I recall her striding out the gate on Coulter St, kicking a pebble before her, her hands jammed into the pockets of her plaid coat. She scowled. "I'm just down at the dobbers," she'd say.

If you're going to say 'shit,' maintain your lady-like composure. A friend of David's told him, "Mrs. Rankin is the only woman I know who can say 'shit' and still be a lady."

"Close the door when you go into the bathroom!"

And "close the sink drain if you're going to clean your ring! Don't want to lose it like Donna did!" She's right. I lost my garnet ring down the drain out at the ranch one summer when I was home from school. Now I close the drain, too, when putting on earrings.

"Stand up straight. I'd like to be proud of you."

Children are to be seen, not heard. Well, that's pretty extreme. I was over 60 when I finally adamantly stated to Mike Shaw, "I will be heard!" That made him very upset.

Have protein for breakfast. She spread cottage cheese on toast.

If you feel uncomfortable when saying goodnight to a boy, ask him in for hot chocolate and cookies.

She showed us this: If you think your house is going to burn down, place your favorite china in the ashes of the clean-out that's in the basement below the fireplace. In 1936, when we lived on Coulter Street in Coquille, an out-of-control forest fire threatened to burn the town. Mother carefully wrapped her favorite china in wet dishtowels and buried the bundles in the ashes of the clean-out receptacle. She also filled the Easy Washer with water, submerged other treasures and put on the lid. Our house didn't burn. But she was ready. As a matter of fact, friends from Bandon, which did burn, brought the few possessions they'd been able to retrieve, usually from their front hall closets. We had fur coats, golf clubs, Christmas lights, and an empty birdcage stashed under the piano in the corner of the living room.

"It's easier to put clean sheets on a twin bed if you stand at the foot of it, instead of at the side. Just flap the sheets over the length of the bed, then the blankets, and tuck them in. Then you can walk to the head of the bed to straighten the bottom sheet and plump up the pillow." I thought Mother's way was a good one and said so in Eighth Grade Home Ec class. The teacher disagreed and told me my mother didn't know what she was talking about. I went home to tell Mother and she shrugged, "That teacher is just a dumb-bunny."

"Oh, there's no time like the present, Daisy Mae!" she'd sing to the tune of "She'll Be Comin' Round the Mountain" as a reminder to not procrastinate.

Save almost everything and you'll have to develop a keen memory. Or never be able to find what you need.

A trick I learned from Mother: If you live in a small house and are having a large group of people in, fill the washing machine with ice and beer. "When the party's over, just take out the leftover beer, close the lid, and put it on spin."

"As long as we can keep laughing, we'll be ok." This she said to Pop when he was rapidly aging and becoming dependent. One afternoon she was helping him to the bathroom when he felt himself losing control. He grabbed the front of his pajama bottoms, which only caused him to spray the wall, the floor, and the hall rug. "Awh, Gawd, look what I've done," he groaned. She held on around his waist and replied, "Oh, hell, Pop, just let it go. What difference does it make?" So he did and they laughed so hard, they both had to lean against the wall.

Give while the Season of Giving is yours. This Mother got out of The Prophet. When she checked into The Siuslaw Care Center, her final address, she told us, "All I need is my toothbrush, my hairbrush, my chapstick and my family." She asked brother David, his wife Dianne and me to prepare for The Grandmother Rankin's Great Big Giveaway. We did and I learned from her to shop in my own home for family gifts.

I still hear you, Mother.

Tell Me a Story

Christmastime, Again!

It's December 15, 2003, Christmastime again! A time of long memories, recognition of changes, joys and pains, connections between then and now.

A few weeks ago, two doors away, at the corner of Garnet and Prospect Streets in Capitola, the house and plants were pushed over and the lot leveled in preparation for a new owner to build a new house. The enormity of the demolition of Old Anna's home echoed within watchful neighbors. We stood in the street transfixed and mute. The yellow monster claw gripped the edge of the roof and crumpled it like a soda cracker. The chimney was toppled, the bedroom wallpaper was exposed, the toilet lifted to the debris truck. Anna's flowers, shrubs, and trees were uprooted. Some of us who had been watching the destruction moved into action, got our clippers and collected holly branches from the downed and doomed tree. Anna would have liked sharing. I got lots.

In the corner kitchen of my small home, I climbed up and down the step-stool, clippers in one hand, branches in the other, dripping rainwater on the counters and floor. I poked the holly branches among the old yellow mixing bowls lined above the cupboards. In other parts of the house, holly nestled between baskets on the tops of the bookcase and china cabinets, along the top shelf of the Santa Claus collection.

But I needed more than holly. When I called a friend who lives in the Santa Cruz Mountains to ask for redwood or pine or whatever she has, all I got was her answering machine. Leaving a message, impatient, I stepped out onto the front porch, clippers again in hand, to scan the neighborhood for a cypress tree or something. I heard the whine of a chainsaw! It seemed close-by. Yes! One block over and around the corner, a huge pine tree was being taken down and the young men were happy to let me have an armload. The pine with the holly helped. The next day when Diane, having heard my message, came down from Felton, she brought Douglas fir branches, which I added.

Stepping back to admire the effect, I thought of long-ago years. I recall this tradition of decking the halls in the house on Coulter Street in Coquille where my brothers and I were children. Of course in Oregon we had endless supplies of greens. Mother sat, protected in a wool plaid jacket and warm pants, on the top porch step, choosing from a mound of Douglas fir, pine, cedar, and myrtle. Flapping the fragrant branches into position, she wound wire to make a thick, heavy swag. "Here," she commanded, "you hold it and hand it up to me." She balanced on the stepladder, fished nails from her jacket pocket, gripped the tack hammer, and attached the swoops across the entire front of the house. Then with muttering and puffing, she twined in strands of colored lights. Over the windows, around the door, into the lattices at the ends of the porch where in another time of year Cecil Bruner roses climbed. I plugged in the lights. "There!", Mother said from the sidewalk, "that looks nice."

Our house on Coulter Street was festive, full of light and life, inside as well as out. Holly and greens on the mantle. Gold sparkling 12-inch snowflakes Mother had made in craft class. A glass bowl of ornaments on the polished grand piano. Ceramic figures of carolers on the buffet. Sets of electric candles along the windowsills.

The nine-foot tree was wired up to an eye hook screwed into the ceiling, so when the Australian shepherd Bootsie chased one of the cats up the tree, it would only swing a little, not tilt over onto Mother's desk in the corner. The Douglas fir Pop brought home from the ranch outside of town was hours fresh, but sometimes lop-sided or scraggly on one side. Mother bored holes with her hand drill in the trunk and inserted extra limbs until it satisfied her artistic eye. She put on the lights and directed us in placing the ornaments, ice cycles, little cardboard houses with cellophane windows, strings of beads, cranberries and popcorn, and finally tinsel. Pop stood near the fireplace, his scotch in hand, and every year proclaimed, "It's the prettiest tree we've ever had!"

Decembers in Coquille were wet and cold. We kids played in the house. With new roller skates, I learned to balance around the dining table. Brothers John and Richard set up an involved electric train that ran behind the sofa, under the piano, across the rug in front of the fireplace and beneath the heavily decorated tree.

90

Sometimes Mother went into our parents' bedroom and shut the door. Sometimes she'd shut the kitchen door, only to open it again and shout, "You kids'd drive a woman to drink!" John and I, on our knees playing train, looked questioningly at each other and rearranged the tracks.

Times change. I don't even have a tree this year, but then, I'll be spending Christmas with my four grown, graying sons and their families.

All I need are traditional greens. Gone are the days when Mother sent an old suitcase of greens on the Greyhound bus. She did that for about 15 Decembers during the 1950's and 60's. She told me Bill Barrows, who owned the Drug Store with a Greyhound Bus bench near the front door, had said that she kept the depot open with her sending suitcases of holly, cedar and fir to my brothers' families and to mine. When the suitcase came to us, we emptied it, filled it with Christmas gifts and sent it back only to have it return full of gifts for us. After the first of the year, I'd fill it with bright California mimosa branches and pussywillows, promises of spring to be enjoyed in the dark days of Oregon winters.

This house doesn't miss a tree at all. It is decked, decorated and ready for the family Christmas caroling. The caroling is my favorite event of the season. The Saturday before Christmas my four sons, Matt, Sam, John, and Marty, their wives, children, some parents-in-law will come for the evening. We wear red sweaters, hug each other, listen to someone read The Night Before Christmas from the book Matt was given 50 years ago. We eat. Grandmother Rankin's Crab Soup is spooned from Christmas mugs. This year will be the 32nd consecutive year we've sung, and isn't it a wonder that we are not any better now than when we started.

We began because John and Marty, still in high school, had a little orange Datsun pick-up truck. The license frame said WE HAUL. They usually hired themselves out to help people clean up their yards or garages. The week before Christmas 1971, they were asked to haul an upright piano from one house to another. They picked it up late Friday afternoon and would deliver it the next morning. It sat up in the truck parked in our driveway. John came into the house, got a kitchen chair, climbed into the truck, and began to play.

What a great idea! Marty and I got some cordwood and the boys wedged the piano in tightly.

They called a couple of fellow high school band members. I called Bill Lee. He offered to drive. We toured, playing and singing for friends who invited us in. Elsa and Peter Mayor offered marijuana brownies.

Our families have been out singing every year since. We have walked around, some with flashlights, some with song sheets, some with old rhythm band instruments, and someone playing guitar. This custom began when we lived in Hillsborough on Brewer Drive and continued later in San Mateo Park, and now in Capitola.

One Christmas over 20 years ago, while Sam and Jane and their infant son Derek lived in Eugene, and Marty was in law school in Salem, John and I drove up and we sang in the freezing cold. A man answered his door, greeted us, hollered for his family to come out, told us to not go away, and went back into the house. In a moment he emerged with his tuba to play along with Sam's and Marty's guitars. Derek awakened, fussed, and Jane sat right down in the snow to nurse him. John thumped the tambourine as I jingled the bells to a fine jazzy rendition of "Santa Claus is Comin' to Town."

Another year we sang at a house where people were partying. A woman came out offering us a plate of cookies. A boy about 10 ran out with an opened bottle of red wine. John accepted it, took a taste and turned to Matt, "Hey, this is a very good, very expensive wine. Quick before his father finds out!"

I recall a precious moment from 1989. Marty's wife, Janet, carrying their bundled thirteen-month-old Roxanne, paused in the middle of the street and tipped Roxanne back, holding her face up. "Look, Sweetie, see the stars. They are always there. Little lights. Like the Three Kings saw."

Roxanne is 15 now. She brings her saxophone. John and Holly's three daughters bring their flute, clarinet and recorder. Sam and Marty still bring their guitars. Maybe Sam's daughter Caitlin will have one of her drums. We will miss Derek. He's grown and living in New York. Matt and Joan's eight-year-old Jamie will bring her keyboard and I'll ask John to play. Maybe I'll rent an orange Datsun truck.

I Said No

Last month I had to say No when Joan asked me to stay with their nine-year-old Jamie. Joan is a thoughtful, loving daughter-in-law, who asks with respect and plenty of lead time. She knows I love Jamie with her bright ideas, fragrant sunshine hair, and solid grip when she holds my hand. I usually am eager to say Yes. But this time I had to say No and I felt sad; not guilty, but remorseful.

Not guilty as I did when Sam called from the florist shop. It was a long time ago, in the late 1960's, when he called from his after-school job at The Flamingo Florist on Broadway in Burlingame, and asked, "Mom, could you come give me a ride home?" I was busy as usual, and answered, "What's the matter with your bike?" He said, "I can't ride it." So, I, the tough mother, replied, "You'll just have to work it out, Sam." When he arrived home on foot an hour later, he was carefully balancing a flower arrangement with a thick yellow candle in the center. "Happy Mother's Day, Mom!" he grinned. I have the candle 35 years later, and still feel like crying in appreciation whenever I think of his generous thoughtfulness. And guilt at not having handled his request better.

I made the same mistake with John. "So, Mom, can you come?" In the early 1970's he was a junior at Northwestern University in Evanston, Illinois, and called to proudly announce he had been chosen to play the triple-drums in the marching band. Northwestern had a pretty poor football team and an award winning marching band, which was to perform during half time in the Northwestern-Notre Dame game. He explained that he wouldn't be able to sit with me, but he'd get me a ticket. I thought of the miserably cold, gusty wind off Lake Michigan during October, the cost of the flight, John's brief half-time performance among musicians who all looked alike in their uniforms, and said, "No, John, not this time." I missed a chance to share in his proud pleasure.

Yes, even missed a chance to live vicariously. When I was a sophomore at Coquille High School, the band received new, shiny copper tympani drums and I yearned to learn to play them. "Puleeeze, Mother, let me join the school band!" I pleaded. "No," she had replied. "It's not necessary. You come right home from school and help with the ironing." My after-school job was to iron napkins, tablecloths, dishtowels, socks and underwear for a family of six. Mother had a mangle, which was a large padded roller with a concave hot metal pressing plate that smoothed everything fed into it. I sulked for weeks. I hated that mangle. When I'd finally grown up, married and had babies in rapid succession, Mother gave us the mangle. I stacked diapers on it and left it when we outgrew the house on Hobart Street in San Mateo.

When son John was a teen-ager, he joined the San Mateo High School Marching Band and played drums. In the symphony band he was in the percussion section and sometimes played the shiny copper timpani drums. I never missed a performance.

Last weekend, November 13. 2004, John and Holly invited me to come watch the Los Altos High School Marching Band in which their daughter Sarah plays the piccolo. It was a bright November afternoon as Sarah's mother Holly and I sat in the bleachers and tried to keep track of Sarah as the band performed intricate marching patterns. As a finale, the band invited family members down onto the field to learn the steps. Sarah pointed to me and I climbed down to join her. She took my hand. "Gran, you take small steps, go 18 steps diagonally, turn like this, again, then 12 steps this way. Turn. Repeat in the opposite direction." She led me again through the maneuvers. "Now," she said, "the band will stand right over there and play while you march."

After more than 60 years I was finally with the band. Not marching quite perfectly, but right there, stepping back and forth across the 50-yard-line and not crashing into anyone! Look, Mother, I've joined the band! The No finally had turned into a Yes.

I said Yes to Mike in 1990 when he asked me to marry him. I hadn't liked the job description for wife, but I wanted to be with him and he said, "The only way for us to be together is to be married." I knew my mother would be pleased. She had always liked

Mike. Indeed, she was grateful to him for "taking care of Donna." Like I was a cat or a bird whose owner had gone away for a week. Mike and I had been good friends for almost 40 years by the time we married in our mid-sixties. I trusted that the friendship quality would endure. I was wrong. He wanted a wife to love, honor and obey him. I loved him. Honored him. I didn't obey. In 2002, after almost 11 married years, he asked me to leave. He wanted to stay on at the country place we shared in southwestern Oregon. I could have the Capitola Cottage. I again said Yes to him. He answered, "All right! You have two weeks to be out of here." "No! No! It will take the entire summer to pack up all this furniture and my belongings. I'll leave Labor Day." I wandered out to the fragrant orchard, along the pasture fences, through the garden, down by the river. The serenity of the country calmed my turmoil. At least we had reached an agreement quietly. I had said Yes and No in the same conversation.

Another time I said No to him and then changed it to Yes. During a California Christmastime visit in 1995, we made an offer on the Capitola Cottage and left to go back up to Oregon. We returned to Capitola in February to sign the papers and as we walked out of the real estate office, Mike said, "Ok. You have two weeks to furnish it as a rental." "No," I laughed, "it usually takes me two years to make the house complete." But I went out and started buying furnishings. A few days later I came home elated and announced. "I can do it! I can furnish the house in two weeks. All I have to do is spend $1,000 a day!" He blanched, but just then a truck pulled up and the men unloaded a washer/dryer, a refrigerator, and a sofa. In two weeks, the house was ready to rent during the months we would not be using it.

With each succeeding year, Mike and I returned to Capitola for the holidays and I stayed on a little longer and a little longer during winter months. By the end of the summer of 2002, I had left the Oregon place in the country to Mike and Capitola became my permanent home. It is filled with sentimental treasures. The yellow candle from Sam is on top of the corner bookcase by the dinner table as a reminder to say Yes.

And Here's Jamie!

"Dear Mom," an email in February 2004 said, "could you take Jamie from late afternoon Friday, February 13, to about noon the 17th? Joan and I need to go to Las Vegas. I could bring Jamie over Friday and Joan could pick her up Tuesday. Love you, Matt."

I replied, "Yes. Will you stay to dinner?" He would.

Matt was bringing energetic, precocious, eight-year-old Jamie from their home in Morgan Hill to stay four overnights. I cancelled a luncheon, a couple of Curves sessions, coffee with Sue Struck and made a list: milk, eggs, bacon, more oatmeal, chunky peanut butter, pears, apples, bananas, popcorn. Another list: Seymour Center, Butterflies, Roaring Camp Railroad, Seeds of Change book store, beach, Katie-Down-the-street. Friday afternoon I stood at the refrigerator. "Hmmm. Thaw some chicken. Boil some potatoes. Jamie can make mashed potatoes. Matt'll like those beans. Ah, here are some carrots and celery." I gathered silverware and napkins to set the table. With my hands still full, I sat down and thought long thoughts.

Jamie is my youngest grandchild. She is a miracle. Daughter of a miracle. In 1952 Jim and I were ready to have children. My father was current President of the Oregon Medical Association and drove around the state to meetings. In January 1953, I wrote, "Dear Pop, If you in your travels run across someone you'd like for your first grandchild, we are ready to adopt."

I continued going to the doctor for tests-to find out what was wrong with me. That is, until summer when, discouraged by the entire process, just stopped. One Saturday morning in August, I stepped into our St. Matthew's Episcopal Church in San Mateo. Only the alter guild lady was there, arranging flowers. I sat. The sun streamed through the stained glass windows just like in religious paintings. I noticed the dust motes dancing just like in movies. I heard only distant outside sounds; traffic, birds, a thump or two. I spoke silently, "Ok, God. I always wanted to be a mother. I grew up preparing for motherhood. Even majored in psychology to help me understand family dynamics. But if you want me to do something else, just let me know and I'll do it. You decide and let me know, ok?"

The following Monday noon Pop called. "I found one. What do you want to do?"

"Oh. Well, uh, Pop, Jim is right here, home to lunch. Let us talk about it and I'll call you back." Tuna sandwiches forgotten. Milk gulped. I returned his call in about ten minutes. "Yes! " I chirped. "Perfect! A boy? I'll fly up tomorrow! When was he born?"

"Saturday morning." Pop replied and not knowing the added significance of Saturday morning, said, "I'll have him here tomorrow afternoon."

I could hardly sleep Monday night. I was dazed by the immediate answer from God. Suddenly I visualized the stone wall around the churchyard and the brass plaque with the church name, Episcopal Church of St. Matthew. I slithered out of bed and felt my way downstairs to the bookshelves to find the old booklet of names and their meanings. Matthew. Gift from God. Back upstairs, I nudged Jim, "I've got the first name! How about the middle name?"

"Give him mine." Jim rolled back to sleep. Matthew Torrance Love.

Tuesday afternoon Mother met my plane as it landed in North Bend, Oregon. She drove us the 25 miles to Coquille and we rushed into the living room of their home. There Pop sat on the sofa. In his left hand, Time magazine. His right hand rested on the bundle of blue snuggled at his hip. "Did you bring the milk? This boy's hungry. No? Well, I'll go get it. You'll want to use only Carnation canned milk. From cows in the spring, full of green grass. Best canned milk there is. Donna, you hold the baby. Ma, you boil the bottles."

Pop stood up and handed me the baby. "Kind of overwhelming, isn't it. Better sit down, Sis."

Rather quickly, more sons were born to us. Sam was delivered when Matt was eight-and-a-half months old. John arrived 16 months later, and Marty 19 months after John. By the time he was four, Matt had three younger brothers. He was serious, responsible, logical, organized. He grew to be an achiever in academics, sports and music. In high school, he and Joan Ferguson dated for two years. She encouraged him to run for Senior Class President. Campaign signs appeared in the hallways. "Love is All You Need", "Love, Love, Love", "Love Makes the World Go Round." He won. She became class secretary. They were a good team.

As difficult as it was to leave her, Matt went 3,000 miles away to Yale. Joan entered San Jose State. Jim and I had separated. Her parents were divorcing. At San Jose State Joan met Dan who said he'd take care of her. She agreed and broke Matt's heart. That summer of 1972, he stared off into space, into the fireplace, out the window. He went to work, sat in front of TV, slept and went to work the next morning. In the fall he returned to New Haven.

During Christmas vacation his senior year, Matt went out on a blind date with Barbara. She was petite, blond, porcelain. She and Matt married 18 months later. She was afraid to have children. He got a vasectomy.

Fifteen years later Matt helped plan the Class of 1971 San Mateo High School 20th Reunion. Joan received an invitation on which Matt had written, "I hope you'll come." She came from Colorado; her husband stayed home. Matt and Barbara drove up from San Jose. As Joan tells it, "Matt and I danced the last dance together. The next day at the picnic we talked. Nothing serious, just old friends. When I got back to Colorado, I wrote Matt to thank him for his part in a great reunion. We started writing to each other once in a while, all casual, for a couple of years."

Meanwhile, Barbara asked me, her mother-in-law, to lunch and cried, swore, threatened and cried some more. "Our marriage is not what I thought it would be," she wailed. They ultimately divorced. By 1993, Joan and Dan divorced. Matt spent time in Colorado. Joan visited in California. In August, 1994, they, each 41, married in the terraced garden of his father's house at Tahoe. I, mother of the groom, choked back tears of gratitude as I stood to say, "When Matt and Joan were dating in high school, they were a terrific couple, but their timing was off. Now, all these years later, they are finally really together!"

Matt surprised and delighted everyone at the wedding when he stood with the band to belt out John Denver's "Home Grown Tomatoes." Losing his usual reserve, he presented to me a t-shirt with tomatoes on the front and one to the father of the bride. He and Joan had chosen that day to recognize Franklyn and me for growing heirloom tomatoes! I was still laughing when Matt danced with me. He swung me out and I reminded him, "You sing and you dance! Even a better dancer now than when you won first prize at Mr. Kitchen's dancing school in Eighth Grade." He danced around with Joan's nine-year-old daughter, Molly. The bride and groom danced with everyone. Matt gazed at Joan, grinning, grinning all the while.

A few months later, Matt called to say, "Mom, I had the vasectomy reversed. It worked. Thirty percent chance of success and I've got swimmers!" One Spring afternoon, he got off the commuter train in Morgan Hill and Joan met him. She held a clutch of pink helium balloons. They called to see if I would come help in October.

I met Jamie Marie Love October 27, 1995. She was two days old, a long blond hungry baby, who except for her pink blanket, looked just like her father at the same age.

One evening that week, Joan was asleep upstairs while in the living room, I watched as Matt held Jamie lengthwise on his lap. His hand covered her tummy much as Pop's had covered his. I watched as he spoke to his daughter, "Now, Jamie, when you get bigger, will you go fishing with me? I'll teach you basketball. We can go kayaking and run the Colorado River."

"Matt," I interrupted. "Do you realize Jamie is the first blood relative you've met?" We were both stunned to tears. In the silence, Jamie pooped.

I snapped out of my reverie, forks still in my hand. I finished setting the table just as footsteps sounded on the front porch. Matt opened the door and called out, "Mom, here's Jamie!"

Look in the Drawer

I opened the junks drawer in my son John and Holly's kitchen. Rubber bands, scotch tape, scissors, odd bits, and, yes, a wooden clothespin.

The kind with the metal spring. Exactly what I was looking for! I twirled the end of the bread wrapper, clipped on the clothespin, and put the bread away in the refrigerator. A clothespin is quick, efficient, re-usable. Much better than those skittery wire twistums and a hundred times better than the plastic notched disk that comes on the sleeve of store-bought bread.

We, my younger brothers and I, learned from our mother the many uses of wooden clothespins. They were probably invented during her young housewife days in the mid-twentieth century by a practical genius who used ash wood and metal clamps. A step beyond the two-legged all wood version my Grandmother Taylor kept in a fabric bag hanging on a nail near her back door.

One of my girlhood jobs was to bring in the wicker basket of fresh, stiff, wind-dried laundry off the line. I set the basket on the bench in the kitchen. Mother filled a Ginger Ale bottle with water, added the perforated top, laid the pieces one-by-one on the table, and sprinkled all the clothes. Wadding them, she stuffed the dampened mass into a pillowcase, twisted the neck, snapped a clothespin to hold it, and popped it all into the refrigerator until time to iron. At the end of the kitchen counter the square glass jar with the yellow metal lid sat full of clothespins.

My brother John and I used to clip them onto our shirt sleeves and pant-legs and pretend we wore fringed Indian outfits. The jar would be empty as we grabbed our bows and arrows and whooped around beneath the back yard apple tree in a war dance. Mother came squinting out into the morning sunshine, stood on the back porch, and pointed into the jar.

Vanquished, John and I returned the pins and thought of something else to play. If we made a sideshow, we needed other clothespins to hang blankets on the lines out near the sandbox, in a sunny corner behind the garage. We put up a sign on the front gate,

"See a real Swimming Match! Pay One Penny!" Peek through a hole in the blanket. Only a wooden match floating in a saucer of water. Neighborhood kids fell for it summer after summer! We also sold lemonade made of the juice of three lemons, a cup of white sugar and five cups of water. If our customers complained too much about the Swimming Match, we gave them free lemonade.

I remember the heavy cast-metal grinder Mother used to make the meatloaf mixture. She kept the various disks together in a small cloth bag, clothes-pinned to the handle. She didn't like to waste time looking for lost parts. On the door of a kitchen cabinet, she tacked a clothespin to hold her recipe up off the counter. On the back porch the tops of the bags of birdseed, dog food and cat kibbles were folded over and clamped with clothespins. In her closet, Mother attached her skirts to hangers with clothespins. They were everywhere in our house!

John and I made rubber band shooters by taping a clothespin to a piece of kindling wood. We stretched the rubber band back from the tip of the stick to the grip of the pin, and hid down behind our white picket fence. When an unsuspecting neighbor kid walked by, we let him have it. Such glee!

John clipped pages together with a clothespin to mark his place in a book. He also figured out that he could break a clothespin apart to use one wooden piece as a shim to level a table. He grew up to become an excellent photographer. Some of our best family photos are from John. He developed large black and white prints in the bathtub and hung them with clothespins to dry.

When our sons were young boys, there were seven of us around the dinner table. I wrote names on clothespins to assign napkins so they could be used more than once. I still find some labeled Chris or Dieter, Remelde, or Elizabeth, all College of San Mateo foreign students who lived with us one at a time, on Brewer Drive in the 1960's.

Occasionally I hold an old clothespin and wonder where those students are now. Today they would be sixty years old! A whole lifetime since I've last called them to dinner.

Clothespins help organize papers, bills, all things pending, awaiting my attention. If I use paper clips, the bundles of papers lie in neat stacks and are forgotten. A wooden clothespin sticks out and demands attention. Sometimes I write a word on the wooden shank as a reminder of the contents.

In the summer of 1996, 40 relatives came for the weekend to Mike's and my farm near Elkton, Oregon, to celebrate our fifth wedding anniversary. I rented pavilion tents and tables and chairs, made green and white gingham tablecloths and looked around the house for something to use as weights. The wind comes up along the Umpqua River in the afternoons and I didn't want the cloths flapping off the tables.

In the potting shed I found some copper wire; in the garage, some eight-ounce fishing weights. In a kitchen drawer lay lots of wooden clothespins. The weighted clips didn't look very sophisticated, but worked fine. I still have some and have included them in making an enclosure of plastic shower curtains hung along a rod on the side the house here in Capitola. The woodpile and gardening table are protected from slanting rains. The wooden pins have darkened with weather and age, but are still firm and functional. They have outlasted Mike's and my marriage.

The tradition of using clothespins may outlast us all. In kitchens belonging to Rankins and Loves, the junks drawer holds wooden clothespins with metal springs. Last month eight-year-old granddaughter Jamie came to ask, "Gran, do you have any clothespins? I'm making a tent." I pointed to the drawer. Out in the yard near the picket fence of my house above Monterey Bay, she fastened beach towels together.

Celebrating Jenny

Jenny is one of my granddaughters, John and Holly's middle daughter. She was almost 13 and the women and girls in our family came together at my house in Capitola May 22 and 23, 2004, to welcome her into womanhood. Eleven of us this time. One other grandmother, three daughters-in-law and six of the eight granddaughters. Sandra, who is my son Sam's wife, and her nine-year-old daughter Indie came from Santa Rosa. They picked up Sandra's mother Betty in Danville. Joan, Matt's wife, and their eight-year-old Jamie came from Morgan Hill while Holly, John's wife, brought their daughters, Sarah who is 15, Jenny, and Katie, 10, from Los Altos. We missed Roxanne, my youngest son Marty's 15-year old daughter. Also missing was Joan's daughter Molly, who is at UNC in Colorado. However, Sam's daughter Caitlin, who at 22 lives in Portland, could be with us.

Isn't it amazing that I have three brothers, four sons, one grandson and eight granddaughters!

Caitlin is the eldest. Several years ago Caitlin and I went to lunch in Santa Cruz and after we'd ordered, she blushed and stated, "Gran, I know what I want to be." I waited. "I'm going to be a world class girl rock drummer!" I didn't know anything about rock bands except glimpses on TV. Where would she go to school to learn that? She didn't go to school. And guess what. She's in two groups. One called Desert City Storm is three boys and Caitlin. The other, I forget its name, is made up of three girls. They travel throughout the United States and have a European tour planned for August. The girl group came to stay over with me a couple of weeks ago on their way to Los Angeles to play. Not models for Nordstrom, they were nonetheless nice girls; respectful, polite, well-spoken, good humored. I was relieved to meet them.

I love having Caitlin around and we all appreciated her effort to be present for our Celebration of Jenny.

A friend lent me a drum. I found all the candle stubs I'd saved, got out the sage stick as well as the rattle made from a dried kelp bulb.

I bought eleven individual pizza crusts and made toppings to please any taste. Also, miraculously, a couple of weeks ago, Barbara-Across-the-Street told me they'd be gone and we could use their beds. That was great, as I'd thought we'd have to erect a couple of dome tents in the front yard. My house is only 1100 square feet.

For Saturday, I had prepared a little light ladies' lunch of tea sandwiches, cherries (Caitlin's and Sarah's favorite fruit), blueberries (for Katie, Indie and Jamie), and lemonade. Joan brought strawberries. As they arrived, I hung a ribbon threaded through an abalone disk around each neck and got a hug in return. We ate right away and then I asked Jenny if she'd like to purify the house.

When we celebrated Caitlin, I hadn't yet thought of smudging the house, but when Sarah and Roxanne were celebrated together, Sarah really liked carrying that smoldering sage stick to all the corners of the house.

The house was thoroughly purified. She likes to lay and light fires and lights all the candles. She likes fire. It was Sarah's idea to get a fireplace in Capitola Cottage. She was about nine one December when she said, "You should have a fireplace right there. All you see out that window anyway is your neighbor's meter box. It'd be lots better to have a fireplace." So now I do.

Jenny is a cautious and careful girl. She held the lighted sage stick over a scallop shell as she led Katie, Indie and Jamie to all the rooms. They didn't take long. When they were through, I asked Jenny to stand in the center of our circle. I shook the painted dried kelp bulb rattle all around her, from her head down to her feet. She stood very still and said yes, she felt blessed.

Jenny rattled Sarah, Sarah chose Katie, Katie did Indie, Indie chose her mother, who did her own mother who did me, and so on until we were all blessed.

Months ago, I had emailed Jenny to ask some of her favorites, so I knew her color is yellow, her flower is the pansy and her birthstone is pearl. I went to The Orange Blossom on Capitola Avenue and asked the owner, Amber, who creates lavish garden hats, to make a headpiece for Jenny. We chose some materials; a pale green garland of small leaves, delicate paper pansies, silk pastel ribbons. I remembered a strand of pearls, not real, but nice, from my Grandmother Sarah Dallas and went home to get them so they could be included. On Saturday when I crowned Jenny, I thought Holly would weep with delight. Jenny with long, glossy, blond hair hanging straight down her ballerina back, glowed as she received our admiration. A magical, mythical princess, even in her levis and t-shirt.

Then it was time to walk the labyrinth. We were quite a parade going outside and around the corner of the house to the side yard. I made a little speech about feeling centered, saying a prayer of gratitude for our love of each other, and especially for Jenny.

Caitlin beat low thunder rolls on the drum as the rest of us walked the labyrinth. I think Indie was the first one through and she played the drum so Caitlin could take her turn. It wasn't a very serious walk; much giggling and jostling as we passed each other coming in and going out. Joan asked, "Does it work if you laugh?"

We came into the house and I escorted Jenny to a chair. As if on a throne, she sat and her family brought gifts. Almost as soon as Indie and Jamie had arrived, Indie had come to ask, "Gran, do you have some ribbon? Jamie and I need some." Now I knew why. They brought to Jenny a pretty bouquet of my garden flowers tied with a ribbon. Others presented their gifts and Jenny carefully, thoughtfully unwrapped each and passed around the cards. A gentle girl-queen accepting homage. Katie reminded us we needed to write the place cards as we'd done last time. With colored pens we each made a name-card for women who influenced our lives and were not with us. Each card was placed near one of the candles on the table.

We had dinner before going to the beach. Sandra had brought·nachos for an appetizer as well as wine. Caitlin opened the packages of Boboli pizza crusts and I brought out all the toppings. Sarah lined up some baking sheets on the counter and everyone made her own. The girls ate the pizzas and we adult women drank wine and made a plan for all our families to spend Christmas together in Mexico. We lighted the candles for the "influential women in our lives who are here because we remember them" and told our stories. I named my mother who almost everyone knew and Mrs. Giddleson who had made me feel elegant when trying on school clothes in her store. Betty told us she and Sandra are from a small family and she's happy to be a part of our large group of relatives. The stories ranged from Katie's pet rabbit that had recently died to Holly's Aunt Mimi who had invited her to tea.

Joan recalled that while in high school she was invited to tea by her boyfriend's mother and felt grown-up. I looked at her through tears. Doesn't seem thirty years ago that she and Matt were dating. Jamie proudly said, "I made a card for Molly. She's my sister in college in Colorado." There were cards for Roxanne. We all felt connected with many women, some of whom we'd never met.

If I were asked what I liked best, I might reply, "Oooh, hard to say. Maybe the way the beach ceremony evolved." A few years ago when we celebrated Sarah and Roxanne, the girls chose to wear large squares of what they call "diaphanous fabrics" that are here for playing dress-up.

Jenny had asked her mother to tell me she didn't want to wear the diaphanous fabrics nor dance. She wanted us just to walk along the beach together. Going to the beach, I'd planned to follow Jenny's wishes. I took one flashlight, just in case. Sandra had brought a basket of small rhythm band instruments, clickers and wooden blocks, small kid stuff, and of course, Caitlin had the drum. Once on the sand, Katie, Indie and Jamie started racing around and pretty soon we all were running and leaping. I set the flashlight upright in a hole in the sand, mainly so no one would fall. Sandra distributed the rhythm band instruments and plopped the basket over the light. Caitlin thumped a rhythm on the drum and the rest of us clicked and clacked along with her. We, after all, danced a circle around our "fire." I watched Jenny. She was into it as much as everyone else, twirling and laughing, flinging her arms up toward the stars and the crescent moon. There we were spontaneously behaving and feeling as women across all millennia and diverse cultures! It was a huge sense of connection for me and I thought that if the girls got an inkling of what it is to be a part of the timeless society of women, this weekend would have been just as I'd hoped. I think that was my favorite moment.

Dinner may have been simple. Dessert wasn't. After we'd walked back from the beach, we trooped out to the back garden, plugged in the strands of outdoor lights and turned on the little water feature. Sarah lighted candles. When we had crowded around the table, Caitlin set the yellow Princess Cake from Gayle's Bakery before Jenny. She cut the first few pieces and then quietly handed me the knife. "Here, Gran. Would you cut the rest?" The conversation seems mostly to have been about cakes. Birthday cakes, cup cakes, wedding cakes, lop-sided cakes, Christmas cakes.

Then it was time to sleep. Caitlin and Sarah got the twin beds upstairs because they had already been admitted to Womanhood. Jenny asked for the couch, saying "I'm elevated from the floor now." I don't know where upstairs the younger three put their sleeping bags as I was about to take Betty, Sandra, Joan and Holly across the street to the neighbors' house. At the last minute, Sandra chirped, "I'm sleeping here on the floor near Jenny," and flapped out her sleeping bag. Everyone had a place and we didn't waken until about eight o'clock. Then, of course, because it's our tradition, we walked down to the restaurant at the end of the wharf. We sat at the center table, the one Jamie calls Our Table.

Sandra, Betty, Caitlin and Indie had to leave by one o'clock so we came chattering back up to the house so we could have time to finish our celebration. Jenny gave each of us a beautifully wrapped fragrant gift. I gave decorated hatboxes to everyone. Inside were a few goodies including some polished stones to remind us we come from Mother Earth. We talked about symbols important in our ritual. Circles of femininity and completion, shells from the sea, the moon, cycles, rhythms of seasons and tides. I noted that the three Stages of Woman were represented among us: Maiden, Mother, and Crone. Holly suggested that we do rites of passage for those emerging from Motherhood toward Cronehood. We agreed to celebrate a year and a day after each final menstrual period.

There was still time to decorate the picture frames Holly had brought. We used pressed pansies, bits of fern, shells, and pearls.

The only mishap of the weekend was Indie's burning herself with the glue gun. She was brave though and seemed recovered by the time we had our closing ceremony on the labyrinth. We stood in a circle and held hands while we each expressed a wish for Jenny. Then we had a big group hug.

One car after another left. I climbed the front steps, sat on the porch to rock and review our time together. I could still feel all the laughter, the silliness, the excitement, and affection. I had said to the daughters-in-law Joan, Sandra, and Holly, "Look at all of us

having this good time and what you initially had in common is only that you married brothers." Joan had laughed, "Yeah, and so?"

And so the granddaughters know they have women in addition to their mothers who love and care for them and would gladly be a resource when needed. And so, as a friend said, "Jenny is looking forward to her moons."

I Bought a Car Yesterday!

Yes, yesterday, July 12, 2004, I bought a car! An extraordinary process for me. Makes me think I've come a long way.

Not until a couple of years after Jim Love and I separated in 1971 and I was 44, did I face a car salesman. Two of our sons were already away at school but John and Marty were still at home, attending San Mateo High School. Two old station wagons sat in the driveway at 735 Brewer Drive in Hillsborough. John and Marty wanted an orange Datsun truck.

We cleaned out one station wagon and drove down to California Drive in Burlingame where a dealer had said, "Yes, we have an orange Datsun pick-up." When we got there, he had a yellow one. No, we wanted orange because San Mateo High School colors were orange and black. We left, disappointed. Eventually, an orange one showed up and we made a deal. The boys did it. I was almost mutely intimidated by the entire procedure. They did all the talking and drove it home, the radio blasting. They got a license frame proclaiming We Haul and earned money with their truck, carried their drumsets around, and got the dog to ride with the wind blowing his ears.

By the time the last son was a senior in high school, I didn't need a station wagon anymore. One day my friend Elaine Cunningham and I were walking down beyond California Drive in Burlingame toward the tennis courts when I saw a brown sedan on the Ford car lot. We stopped to look. The salesman sauntered out of the office and asked if I'd like to see the motor. "No," I said, "as long as it has one." Elaine commented, "It's a nice color. Matches your living room rug." The man asked if I'd like to test drive it. "Not today, but Saturday I attend a class in Palo Alto and I could take it then to see how it drives. I'd have it for a couple of hours." He said that wasn't possible, so Elaine and I walked away to go play tennis. He wrote down my name.

I asked Elaine's husband Lloyd about how to buy a car. He gave me a book titled "What I know about Cars" by Donna Love. It was full of blank pages. He advised me that if a salesman tried to pressure me I should say, "I'll have to talk with my lawyer about your proposal. He takes care of all my affairs." Next day the car salesman called to say I could drive the car Saturday if I'd leave my station wagon with him. That worked. I dashed from the house early Saturday enroute to class. When Marty got up he thought I'd sold the car and raced on his bike to retrieve his homework. Later that day, the fast-talking salesman threw figures and statistics at me and I tried Lloyd's suggestion. The salesman stopped, took a breath, and adjusted his tie. "Now, what was it you wanted?" he asked. I got the original offer on the old station wagon and the price of the new car. I drove that car for more than ten years...and don't remember the model name.

The first car I really fell in love with was a used yellow Toyota pickup with a camper on the back and huge wheels that teenage carryout boys thought was cool. I needed it because in 1987 I had bought a little house in Alamos, Sonora, Mexico and wanted to haul some furnishings from my home in San Mateo. I asked a friend who had been recently widowed if she wanted to drive down with me. "Do you have air conditioning?" she asked. "No, but the windows go up and down." Phyllis agreed and we headed south. Outside of Barstow, the car kept losing speed. It chugged and sputtered more and more slowly and finally I parked off the side of the road in the shade of an overpass out in the Mojave Desert. Phyllis panicked. "Whatever will we do!" She'd led a protected housewife life. I unloaded a chair from the back of the truck and handed her an orange to peel as she sat on the side of the road in the shade. I walked back and forth picking up road trash and trying to decide what to do. When a carful of teenage boys stopped, I asked them to please notify AAA in the next town. Phyllis was on her second orange and our side of the highway was clean when we climbed into the cab of the tow truck to head back to Barstow.

The mechanic at the repair garage said it would be a couple of days before he could get to our truck. We just looked at each other. "Let's go have lunch." We took the owner's manual with us and thumbed through it. We could hardly understand the vocabulary. As Phyllis, mother of five sons said to me, mother of four sons, "Mothers of boys don't do cars." But we continued through the book as we ate. Symptoms were listed along with probable causes. Ah, here it is! We asked the waitress and learned that the nearest Toyota dealership was only a couple of blocks away. The truck probably could make it that far. Yes, the air filter was clogged with dust. We bought two, just in case, and feeling puffed with pride, drove on south without any further problems. I sold that Toyota to a friend in Alamos when I sold the house in 1993.

I must have still had a car at home, although I've forgotten it. In 1991 I married Mike and he does cars. When whatever I was driving began to spend more time in the repair shop than taking me on errands, I said I might need to buy another. Mike eagerly offered to drive to the nearest car lots. I thought I'd like green this time. They didn't have green. They had a grey four-door sedan that Mike recommended so I bought it. My brother Richard laughed, "It's perfect for a funeral procession." I agreed. It was drab as an overcast day, sad, and ol'-lady-looking.

By the mid-1990's, I'd sold my house in San Mateo so Mike and I could move to rural Oregon. We agreed to buy a winter home in Capitola and again I was shlepping possessions back and forth between two houses. One December Sunday, we agreed to go look at cars. At the Ford lot on Soquel Avenue in Santa Cruz, the first thing I saw was a shiny, apple red 1991 Ford Explorer. I wasn't prepared to find something so quickly and didn't even have my checkbook with me. The salesman said he'd hold the car and take the grey funeral car as a trade-in. Mike drove me back to the house and during the return trip said he'd buy the car from me for the same price. Good deal for him, ok with me. That Sunday afternoon I owned the largest vehicle I'd ever driven. Since our legal residence was in Oregon, I applied there for a personalized plate: I wanted Big Red! That was taken. Of course. Every logger in Oregon called his truck Big Red. I settled on CRONE. The woman taking my application asked, "What's a Crone?"

The Explorer gave me pleasure each time I looked at it and it faithfully carried loads of Christmas gifts, our farm harvests, and supplies up and down the highways between Capitola and southwestern Oregon. As Mike's and my marriage faltered, the name Explorer came to label my life. I explored possibilities for my future.

On the road. Life's road. On my own. Again.

But, after all, it was just a car. Like most of us, it grew old and ailing. A few weeks ago my eldest son Matt was visiting and as he parked the Explorer, the key stuck in the ignition. Exasperated, he muttered, "Don't put any more money into this car, Mom."

He was right. A year ago the transmission was replaced. There was a crack in the windshield, the air conditioner didn't work. I had spray painted some dings and scratches with fair success. And now the key was stuck. It turned on and off, so when I got out of the car, I just draped a kitchen towel over the steering column.

Last Tuesday I drove from Capitola to San Mateo to have lunch with Mike's daughter-in-law Jan Shaw who was visiting from Spokane. I noticed that every time I used the brake, there was a grinding sound. If I stepped on the brake quickly, it grabbed. I could hear ominous clanking and rattling. In San Mateo, I drove into a parking lot, got out, and patted the Explorer. "This is it, ol' pal." After lunch Jan and I called AAA, sat on the metal steps at the edge of the parking lot and waited. Two hours! When he finally appeared, the tow truck driver told us the other truck had brake problems as it was coming, so he was called. It was ok. Jan and I had a fine time trading stories about our lives. We hugged goodbye and I climbed up beside the driver. All the way home he told me about vitamins and supplements. Also he said that he rarely tows Nissans, Hondas or Toyotas.

So on Wednesday I rented a car, found the Toyota dealership at the end of 41st Avenue, learned it's possible to see models on line and spent the evening hunched at the computer. Thursday I went down to the Ford place on Soquel Avenue where I'd found the Explorer just to look at colors and to touch various cars. I had a top dollar budget of $20,000. That's with license, tax, tire recycling fees, everything "Out the door" the salesman called it. He had a pretty sea-green 2005 Ford Escape. But over my price. "If you really want the car, if that is the car for you, don't let a few hundred dollars stand in your way." Friday morning I called my son John. John-the-Clear-Thinker. He suggested I look at another Ford agency. "And, Mom, ask a lot of questions. Find out how motivated the dealer is. Ask for what you want and give yourself time to think about it.

Tell Me a Story

Call me if you need to have me talk with him. I know how you can be intimidated by car salesmen." Was he remembering the orange Datsun truck?

I drove the rental car to Moss Landing for a picnic with school-chum Virginia who lives in Carmel. We walked along the beach picking up sand dollars. As we sat on a log to eat our sandwiches, I told her about the perplexities of buying a car. She said she hated buying cars and put it off as long as possible. We talked a long time about our long lives. Two women sitting on a driftwood log on a windy beach talking in timeless fashion. Part of the heritage of being women friends.

That afternoon, driving back toward Capitola, I turned off to Watsonville, found the Ford dealership, pulled in and saw a shiny, apple red Ford Escape. It looked like a baby of the Explorer. An eager young salesman said, "It's a brand new 2003. Has 120 miles on it. Last one on the lot." I told him I liked the color and he opened the door for me to get in. It was so cute! "I'll spend $20,000 out the door." I told him. "We can do that," he said. And so we did. I signed the papers and wrote a check. They gave me a bottle of Martinelli's Sparkling Apple Cider and a jar of locally made salsa as well as many smiles and handshakes.

Raphael, the salesman, followed me home in my new car. Someone else from the agency followed to take him back. I'd bought a car. An Escape! An escape from what? To what? Another new chapter in my life?

Epilogue: I planned to contribute the Explorer to Helping Hands of San Mateo County. I would have except that Katie-Down-the-Street's son Dan thought he wanted it. He decided against driving it as far as Tucson, but Dan's brother Paul definitely wanted it and knows how to fix brakes. He repaired them Sunday and drove home. The Explorer now lives in Amador County where Paul will care for it and with his family, take it on ski trips. Their daughters like it so much they took their sleeping bags out and slept in it.

A Peek at a Part of Alaska

The lowest tide of the year 2004 occurred the last Friday of July. It was minus-26 feet at Petersen's Bay when our Elderhostel Group took a small excursion craft from Homer on the Kenai Peninsula to the Marine Field Studies Center. I was glad I had the walking stick the cabdriver in Anchorage had found in his trunk and offered to me. The birch branch was exactly the right height to steady me among the slippery rocks and muddy sea bottom. Rich life clings here. Me, too. We watched clams spitting small synchronized fountains of water, took picture after picture of sea stars, marveled at sea urchins and all sorts of tide pool creatures before the tide came sweeping back in and we climbed the hill to the Field Research Center to lunch. Later we hiked a trail through temperate rain forest and picked wild blueberries while the naturalist told us of the importance of protection and preservation. Of respect. She was passionate in emphasizing that mankind is a visitor to these lands. We left some blueberries for the bears.

At the Pratt History Museum in Homer, visitors took turns, ten at a time, crowding into a homesteader's cabin to listen to Mrs. Greer, her calico dress and apron perfect for her docent role, her grey hair soft around her sweet face. She told of homestead days, cutting trees to make a cabin, digging a hole for an outhouse, getting to town on frozen winter rivers, a husband killing a moose and hanging it from a tree near the woodpile. During the dark winter, the wife took her ax and hacked off a hunk of frozen meat for supper. Mrs. Greer, not much older than I, was that wife. She and her husband had come after World War II to see Alaska. And stayed. "We just followed our boots," she smiled. I had thought that homesteaders were at least my Grandmother Taylor's age.

Over and over, we heard people say, "I came for a few months and stayed 17 years. There's not only a spaciousness here along with clean air and water, there is an openness and confidence among folks, a naturalness. We live with the rhythm of the tides, the animals, and the weather more than is possible in the lower 48."

My traveling friend Phoebe and I spent some days prior to and following the week of Elderhostel. On a drizzly day, we took the train from Anchorage to Denali. During the guided bus tour on the 89-mile road, the only road within the park, we viewed ten blond grizzly bears, nine moose, 20 dall sheep, 14 caribou, eight yeagers, six ptarmign birds, and an eagle. We learned about braided rivers and kettle ponds. I heard that within the three park and preserve entities of Denali, there is 1 bear per 20,000 acres. Denali is larger than Rhode Island. The guide, who teaches middle school in Healy, told us Alaskans are fighting to keep Denali free of commercialization.

Although Phoebe and I didn't see Mt McKinley, the tallest mountain in North America...so huge it creates its own weather, we did see the famous Aialik Glacier when we took an excursion on Resurrection Bay. The boat pulled up close to the Glacier so we heard the crack and felt the swell when a small chunk fell off. The announcer informed us that the glacier had just calved a piece of ice the size of a seven-story building. The mass of the glacier dwarfs the chunks sliding into the Bay. I was surprised that the glacier field creates fierce wind that pours down onto tourists. We had the same experience when we hiked to Exit Glacier near Seward. The day was sunny and warm, the air still, until we rounded a corner up near the edge of the glacier and the cold wind hit us in the face. We took pictures of the blue crevices and scuttled back down around the corner in among the alders and black spruce. Ground squirrels scampered across our path kicking up tiny swirls of dust.

Iditarod. What a mysterious word. We found out that the word means "far place." A place between Anchorage and Nome where gold was discovered in the early 20th century. The Iditarod Trail was merely the trail upon which dog sleds took mail and supplies and returned with gold. Things change. Now the gruelingly competitive Iditarod Race brings TV fame to scores of determined dog teams and their owners who persevere through continuous hours of sledding. And fame, too, to a far place where the gold ran out.

Not only the gold, but also an ancient way of life is running out. A way in which wealth was not measured by possessions, but by intelligence, bravery, wisdom, family. In Jean Craighead George's

Julie of the Wolves, the young heroine observes, "The old Eskimos were scientists, too. By using the plants, animals, and temperature, they changed the harsh Arctic into a home, a feat as incredible as sending rockets to the moon. The people had not been as outdated and old-fashioned as she had been lead to believe (in the village school). No, they had been wise. They had adjusted to nature instead of to man-made gadgets."

Although Phoebe and I visited only south central Alaska and were there for only 17 days, we are conscious of the changes taking place. From Russian fur gatherers to missionaries, to the pipeline, Alaskans are deeply affected. In Anchorage I bought a soapstone and ivory carving of an Eskimo woman with her drum. She has short arms, true to the warmth-conserving stature of her people. She has a happy smile. She is drumming the joy of her man's return from hunting. I have named her Uma or Alice. She was carved not by a man, as is usual in Point Hope on coast of the Arctic Ocean, but by an Inupiak woman, Edith Oktollik, single mother of two daughters. I don't know why she is a single mother. I wonder what happened to her man. He probably didn't get lost in his kayak when he went out seal hunting. Maybe he was a victim of rampant alcoholism. Edith carved Uma in February of 2003, a dark month, traditionally good for carving. This year Edith has moved to Anchorage so her daughters can get better schooling. She is part of the tides of change, the loss of the old ways.

A Native Alaskan in Seldovia quoted his father's wisdom, "when you're afraid, change something." Edith Oktollik may have been afraid for her daughters' futures. She has made a change. She has followed her boots.

Showed Up and Joined Up

Who, me! In the political scene? Not me. I've proclaimed many times that I'm apolitical, into social causes and charities, but never affiliated with politics. Most of my adult life was lived on the San Francisco Peninsula, a silk shirt and pearls sort of neighborhood, where I volunteered for the Coyote Point Museum Auxiliary, the Family Service Auxiliary, school, church, and Boy Scouts, but nothing political. On the Great Peace March of 1986, I was recognized as a relatively conservative person. Young Marchers brought their worried parents to me to be reassured that not everyone on the March was weird.

This year, 2004, the Bush Administration has me frantic with worry. This year I live in Santa Cruz County. This year I am increasingly aware of my growing-up grandchildren and the world they will inherit. If they live through their draft age.

So, early in October, I showed up at the Democratic Headquarters in the Galleria Building in downtown Santa Cruz and stood to watch the buzz and action of a dozen or so people. Some phoning, some on computers, some sorting papers, some deep in conversation, all looking as though they were enjoying their dedicated team efforts. I saw organized chaos complete with coffee mugs, pretzels, half-eaten pizzas and bags of apples among the piles of posters, pins and stickers all proclaiming the candidates, John Kerry and John Edwards. This must be Democracy in action!

A woman came in the door and was greeted by a young man in jeans and t-shirt. She told him, "I'm bi-lingual. Spanish. Could you use me?" The young man brightened, gave her a list of names and a script as he showed her to a phone. An elderly gentleman came in and announced, "I'm here. Put me to work!" I stepped forward and soon sat at a table to write letters encouraging people in Florida to vote. A man who also was writing letters told me he was over 80 and grew up in Republican Hillsborough at the other end of Brewer Drive where our young family lived in the 1960's. He and I chatted about changing times until I stood up to take with me lists of people who live in Ohio. At home I wrote letters to encourage them to vote with me for Kerry and Edwards.

Later that week when friend Faye called to ask if I'd like to go to Reno to help at Democratic Headquarters, I answered an emphatic YES! Nevada is a swing state, has five electoral votes and needed us. Four of us women, Claire, Florence, Faye and I, drove to Reno last Tuesday, October 12, 2004, and went directly to Democratic Headquarters. A young woman whose name tag said Meagan, greeted us, told us she was from San Francisco, had in fact quit her job to work this year for Kerry. She herded us into a somewhat quiet room and told us how to make phone calls.

We did, for four hours, then left to check into the hotel, The Silver Legacy, right downtown, thirty stories of pulsing neon, valet parking and artificial flower displays as big as my bathroom at home. After we'd freshened up a bit, we walked to 130 West Street to Beaujolais Bistro. Surely it must be one of the best restaurants in Reno. The service, wine and food were excellent. What's more, patrons sitting nearby smiled at us and complimented our Kerry pins. Claire gave hers to a woman who beamed as she pinned it to her sweater. Faye gave hers to the maitre'd who promised he'd put it on right after work.

Next morning we returned to Democratic Headquarters and learned that John Kerry was in Las Vegas. George Bush was to speak in Rancho San Rafael Regional Park in Reno and Laura Bush was at a fundraiser at Glenwood, Lake Tahoe. Teresa Heinz Kerry was in Reno. We had chosen a good week to be in Nevada.

Meagan gave us a map, some lists and sent us out to do door-to-door canvassing. Most of the neighborhoods we saw were poor. Most of the people were not home. The four of us dragged through the lists until late in the hot afternoon, buoyed by the few people who answered their doors, listened, and thanked us for the campaign sign we planted in their scruffy front yards. We finished just in time to drive to "The Wal", a pub across the street from the University of Nevada-Reno campus where locals were to gather for the third Presidential Debate. We squeezed in and found places to perch. Rimming the rooms high above our heads at least 20 TVs were turned on, two to a Boston Red Sox-New York Yankees ball game and the rest to the debate. Wine came in tumblers and there was no way we could be served dinner, but the excitement and comradery obliterated hunger.

As soon as the debate ended, everyone poured out of the pub and down the hill to UNR's Lawlor Events Center. Over 10,000 people lined up debating the Debate in the crisp autumn evening. We were there to see Michael Moore. He waited over an hour for us to find our seats. When he finally shuffled on stage, everyone stood to shout, whistle, stomp and clap. He was rumpled, funny, passionate, intimate. He spoke mainly to the students. He revealed that the major pharmaceuticals won't let him into their buildings for interviews. He asked how many had cell phones. Over half the hands went up. He said, "Turn on your phones, hold them up over your heads." Thousands of small blue lights glowed. As Michael Moore swayed back and forth, so did all the little blue lights. He continued to sway and sang, "All We are Asking is Give Peace A Chance." Then, as though that were not enough, he called out, "I have a phone number for you. I want you to dial it. Now. It is the number for one of those pharmaceuticals. Pretend you are the guard. When someone answers, tell them, 'I saw him. Michael Moore is in the hall. Michael Moore is in the elevator. Emergency! Michael Moore is in the building.'" A young man right behind us called out, "I've got 'em!" Another shouted, "I'm on hold." Another said, "Line's busy!" Michael Moore doubled over and clutched his sides in laughter. I hadn't known that political work could be so much fun!

The four of us women were so elated, we knew we couldn't sleep. Back at the hotel, we each ordered a bowl of soup. When Claire and Florence went up to bed, Faye and I played the slot machines. It took a long time to lose $20.00. That was ok, we had fun and could sleep in a little tomorrow. Tomorrow we were going to the Neil Road Rec Center in south Reno where at 11:30 Teresa Heinz Kerry was to speak.

We arrived an hour early and the parking lot was full. Claire and Florence drove out to park the car while Faye and I went in to find seats. All the seats were taken. I asked a woman who held onto a folded chair where we might find some. She pointed across the room to a small office. We asked the receptionist. She pointed to a tall man who looked important. He pointed to a young woman in a raspberry red blouse. I held onto her arm and again asked, "Where shall we four senior women from Santa Cruz sit today?" She answered, "Follow me. Don't tell anyone. Hide your blue tickets." She led us up to the fourth row, center. The red ticket section.

As we talked with those around us, a familiar looking man edged his way along toward his seat. "Joe!" I cried out and stood up. He blanked for a moment and then, "Donna! Is that you? Do you live up here now?" Joe Broido was on the Peace March. We last saw each other in November, 18 years ago. He told me Dan Chavez, the March attorney, was also in Reno, responsible for the getting-out-the-vote agenda. Indeed, in a few moments, Dan tapped the microphone, made some announcements and introduced the man who introduced the woman who introduced Teresa Heinz Kerry.

She was an average size woman in a tailored black pants suit with a mass of luxurious brown wavy hair that she pushed back out of her pleasant face as she stood to accept our applause. She smiled. Teresa Heinz Kerry seemed to me to be centered, poised, dependable, gracious. Nice. She spoke with quiet assurance; a casual, friendly delivery of facts relating mostly to health care. She said, "We must be responsible for our own health. Exercise. And if you must take prescription drugs, it is not your fault you are made a criminal because you can't afford to pay prices in the United States. Go ahead, get your medications from Canada. Someone will notice and make a change. What's more, sometimes you don't need all those drugs. Someone told me the other day that for arthritis you need to get some white raisins. Soak them in gin for two weeks. Then eat nine raisins each day, preferably in the morning." We wrote down the recipe. A man who was seated on stage, raised his hand. "I am a doctor, have been on state and national AMA boards. I also know something of holistic medicine and can say that raisins in gin are a sound suggestion. The chemistry is similar to what you get in Chondroiton and Glucasamine." Teresa shrugged, "There you have it" We sat in the fourth row, transfixed. She answered questions from the audience until someone reminded her that there was a plane to catch.

After a standing ovation, we joined others to meet our next First Lady. When my turn came, I lightly touched Teresa's wrist to say, "As one doctor's daughter to another, I understand where you learned your compassion." She stopped signing autographs to look up at me, nod in acknowledgement, and murmur, "Yes, we both know."

It was hard for me to leave. I know now what a groupie feels. Was it really after two o'clock? Claire asked, "How about lunch?" Faye turned to a mature woman with a bright face and sleek blond hair pulled smooth. "Oh" she said, "follow me. I'll take you to Austins." She told us about Reno, her home for 33 years. The waitress pinned on the Kerry button as soon as I gave it to her. We hurried through our salads and sped back to Democratic Headquarters where we sat at phones until nine o'clock.

When we pulled into the hotel, the valet, a UNR student wearing the button we'd given him the day before, bounced over to us. "I joined the protest at the Bush speech today! That's the first time for me. Where do I get a Kerry-Edwards sign?"

Next morning we packed and were going down in the elevator when a respectable looking older couple got in. The wife stood modesty, clasped her hands, and looked down. The man noticed my button, shook his head and contorted his face into an expression of disgust. I looked at him until he met my gaze, then smiled and said, "We are so fortunate to live in a country where we can express our choices, aren't we." He gave a reticent little smile and murmured, "Yes, we are." His wife followed him out. Faye gave me a thumbs-up. The woman at the checkout desk wanted a Kerry button. The boy at the coffee stand wanted a button. The girl in the newspaper shop wanted one, too.

We four, Claire, Florence, Faye and I, climbed into the car and headed home. Enroute we decided we're going to make and market Teresa's raisins and gin. If it's ready in time, we'll offer it at the Victory Party on November 2.

I sat in the back seat and realized I was a long way from the years of apolitical silk shirts and pearls.

What's A Groover?

"A groover?" Matt's wife Joan asked as she listened to reports of recent adventures. "What's a groover? Dare I ask?" My son Matt and I laughed as we recalled that I had asked exactly that question when our group of river rafters was getting organized to float the Green River in June of 2002. Eric, one of the guides of Hatch River Expeditions out of Vernal, Utah, called the 15 of us "guests" together and explained River Etiquette.

"Don't crowd other rafts."

"If you fall in, go down stream face up, feet first."

"Take only pictures and leave only footprints."

"And," Eric waved a roll of toilet paper, "we will put this roll on a rock at the head of a trail near our nightly campsites. When you need to, take the paper. When others see the paper gone, they'll know to wait. Go down the path and find the groover."

"A groover? What's a groover?"

"Ah," he smiled. "A groover is an Army Surplus metal Ammo box that has a lid that seals with a rubber gasket. It's our way of leaving only footprints behind. You might notice that when you use it, you'll get grooves on your bottom." Matt and I chuckled.

The system worked well for the four days we floated down river and set up camps on the sandy little beaches. I followed the directions to the groover, taking the roll of toilet paper with me, returning it to the rock or log at the trailhead. It was like locking and unlocking the bathroom door. Guaranteed privacy. So smart to have a groover!

Matt was eager to tell Joan and their seven-year-old Jamie. Then we looked for a surplus store to check out the supply. There were tall stacks of groovers of all sizes! Matt enthusiastically bought several. "They'll make good storage boxes in the garage, Mom," he said.

Several weeks later, in September, members of our families met in Santa Rosa for son Sam and Sandra's wedding. Jamie ran over to me and tugged, "Come 'ere, Gran! See what Dad has for you!"

Matt and Joan opened the trunk of their car and there was an immaculately painted turquoise colored small sized groover! Matt watched my delighted face and said, "Open it." It was full of CD's he'd made for me. I laughed and cried as I hugged him. Jamie carried it to my car. From then on, I listened to music wherever I went.

Exactly a year later, I drove to Oregon and Washington to see family and friends and to collect some of the Northwest's produce. I stopped in Winchester Bay to buy cases of albacore tuna and had driven only a mile or so when I noticed lots of air rushing around in the car. I checked the windows. They were up. I checked the fan. It was off. I looked in the rear-view mirror and gasped as I realized the back of the car was open! Parked off the road, I checked everything. My luggage was there. The cases of tuna were there. An empty cardboard box had tumbled out and was lying back along the side of the road. I sighed in relief and closed down the hatch. In Roseburg I bought boxes of peaches and berries to can when I arrived back home in Capitola.

Toward the end of the week I assembled the canning equipment, turned on the stove and began the happy process of preserving for Christmas gifts, the treasures of my trip. In a moment between stirring and pouring, I decided to play some music. Where had I put the groover when I unpacked? I checked the shelves near the CD player in the house, I checked the bottom of my closet, the car, the luggage storage. The car again. Nowhere! Then with grief I realized it probably was settled in the weeds along Highway 101 just outside Winchester Bay, Oregon.

I felt bereft. The groover was one of my prized possessions. How could I tell Matt!

The next time we were together I admitted my foolish carelessness. He hugged me and sympathized, "Ah, Mom, we all do things we regret. I have lots of groovers and will get another one to you." He did. It's white. And it's filled with more CD's. I keep it in the house, on the shelf near the player.

In July of 2005, I again packed the car for a tour of Oregon. I had gone only 3 blocks when I realized that I'd forgotten to bring some CD's to hear while driving. I turned around the block, dashed into the house, grabbed the groover. Then stopped. Opened it, took out a handful, closed it and put it back on the shelf. All the way up I-5 I sang with Sarah Brightman and on the return trip down 101, belted out songs with Barbra Streisand. When I got home and unloaded the new supply of Winchester Bay albacore tuna, there was the groover sitting on the shelf, safe.

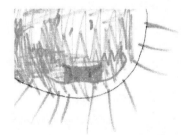

Easter Eve in the Desert

My son John, his wife Holly and their three daughters, ranging in age from sixteen to ten, drove from their home in Los Altos to La Quinta, near Palm Springs, in 2005 for Easter. They were the only ones this year staying at John's father's wife's second home where often multiple relatives gather. It is an elegant place. Spacious. Warm swimming pool. Tennis courts nearby. Golf. The whole Desert Package. A perfect recreational vacation for a busy family. Four days of delicious indulgence.

On the third day Holly took the car to drive to Los Angeles to visit her older brother who lived in a care center. John and the girls remained at the house, played tennis, went to the driving range and had lunch at home. Holly called to say her brother wanted her to stay to dinner. "That's fine. Have fun. See you later tonight," John replied.

He realized, as he hung up, they had nothing in the house to eat for dinner and no car. The youngest daughter opened and closed the refrigerator, then the freezer. "Nothing!" she wailed. "How will we survive?"

The sixteen-year-old rummaged in the pantry. "Pancake mix and some olives." she announced. Of course, they could order pizza.

"Or," the quick thinking thirteen-year-old offered, "we could consider dinner at the clubhouse?"

"They're probably not serving tonight, the night before Easter," the eldest said.

"You may be right but I know how to find out," said John. He and the ten-year-old drove the golf cart the mile to the club. Yes, they would be serving that evening. It was to be dressy.

"Wear your Easter dresses," John suggested. "Oh, but we wanted to save them for tomorrow," the sixteen-year-old sighed. "What are our options?" John asked. "Let's get dressed up and go!" the ten-year-old squealed. John found one of his father's sports coats that fit well enough. They all crammed one on top of the other into the golf cart and arrived at the Club House.

They were back home when Holly returned about nine o'clock. "How was dinner?" she asked. "Lovely!" said the sixteen-year-old. "Elegant!" said the thirteen-year-old. "Great!" said the ten-year-old. "It was memorable," said John.

Next day, they put their dresses on again, John wore the sport coat, Holly wore her pearls. They sat properly in the car and drove to Easter Brunch. They had survived Easter Eve in the Desert!

I Got It Back!

I got it back! My father's wing chair! Would he remember the one he sat in while our family lived on Coulter Street? Mother had seen it one day, in probably 1937, in the window of Purkey's Furniture Store as she was coming out of the post office. Not only for our father, but one for her, too. She went right in, ordered fabric with large deep red cabbage roses and came home to tell him what she'd done. "Sounds good," he said.

Yes, he would remember. He sat in that chair near the fireplace in the evenings throughout my childhood. Sometimes my brothers or I sat in it to read Compton's Encyclopedias. He was sitting in it the evening I anxiously pirouetted in front of him to show off the green taffeta and black lace party dress Mother and I had found that day when we went shopping. I was so relieved when he looked up from his medical journal, nodded approval and said, "You're turning out to be a nice looking girl, Sis."

The tea cart was next to the chair, current magazines on the lower shelf, the blown glass ashtray and pale sculpted cigarette box on the tabletop. Only nine steps from the front door so brother John and I could tiptoe in, reach into the box, grab one cigarette and scamper across the street to sit under Mansel's barn to light up and practice. What a risk we took! Not only at getting caught taking a cigarette, but Mr. Mansel kept their old trucks in the barn and it was saturated with oil and gasoline.

I wrote a children's story* about the wing chair.

> *"Once upon a time on Coulter Street in a small town named Coquille, there lived a man named Jack. He lived with his wife Mildred and their four healthy children named Donna, John, Richard, and David.*
>
> *Each morning Jack went to the office in his hospital. Each evening he came home and said, "I'm tired after working all day." He sat and rested in his big wing chair. He read a medical journal or* Time *magazine.*

> *He did this for many years. His children grew up."*

In about 1944 the his-and-hers chairs moved when our parents went to live on the Ranch five miles out Fat Elk Road. Our father sat in his and gazed out the large picture windows across Coquille Valley. He watched cows grazing in the very bottomland he putted across in the little motorboat toward town when winter floods covered roads and fields. He steered along a fence line, tied up at the Coos Creamery and walked the few blocks to the hospital.

The chairs were in that living room on the Ranch during the reception for Jim Love's and my wedding, Tuesday, August 16, 1949.

Years passed. In 1960 when we, now a family of six, bought the big house on Brewer Drive in Hillsborough, my mother kept her chair and my father gave his chair to Jim and me. The cabbage roses were exchanged for a soft silky celadon that blended with the avocado green sofa and golden wheat colored carpet. Jim sat in it to read. Not our boys. It was designated their father's chair.

> *"Jack and Mildred's daughter Donna married Jim and they had four fine sons named Matthew, Sam, John, and Marty. They moved to a large house. Jack and Mildred said, "Here. The big wing chair is yours now."*
>
> *Each morning Jim went to the office. Each evening he came home and said, "I'm tired after working all day." He sat and rested in the big wing chair. He read The Wall Street Journal and Newsweek magazine.*
>
> *He did this for many years. His sons grew up."*

In 1971 Jim left our home to live alone. He didn't go far. Just down to an apartment complex named Woodlake near San Mateo High School where the three older boys were students. Marty was still an 8th grader at Crocker Middle School. A few years later, the wing chair again moved when I bought the smaller house on Occidental Avenue in San Mateo Park. This time I had it recovered in a rich tobacco colored suede cloth, and set it near the fireplace. By now, the boys were in college. When they finished school, they married. Sam and Jane were the first to have children. When they visited, we sat in the chair to read to their young Derek and Caitlin.

I completed two teaching credentials, had the tutoring service for 15 years, bounced around for a while until I married Mike Shaw in the summer of 1991. He came with two wing chairs. I gave mine to Marty and Janet and their infant daughter, Roxanne.

> "Marty married Janet and they had a bright-eyed daughter named Roxanne. They lived in a large house. One day when Roxanne was three, Donna said, "Here, Marty. The big wing chair that belonged to my father is yours now."
>
> Each morning Marty went to the office. Each evening he came home tired from working all day. He sat and rested in the big wing chair. Do you know what he read?
>
> Did he read a medical journal and Time magazine?
>
> No.
>
> Did he read The Wall Street Journal and Newsweek magazine?
>
> No.
>
> "What shall I read?" he asked.
>
> Roxanne brought him one of her favorite books. She sat on her Daddy's lap. They opened the book. Together in the big wing chair they read a story. Marty said, "Roxanne, let's name this chair. What shall we name it?" Roxanne sat a while in her Daddy's lap. She leaned back close to him. She looked up and said, "I know! Let's name it 'The Reading Chair.'"
>
> And so they did."

Their lives changed. Marty stored the chair in a shed in his dog run. He recently offered it to anyone in the family. No one has room for it.

My life has changed, too. When Mike and I separated in 2002, his wing chairs stayed with him. So on May 7, 2005, I drove up to Marty's house in Marin County to retrieve my father's and brought it directly to a nearby upholsterer's on Soquel Drive.

Now it has pale peachy roses and faces the fireplace in the little living room here in my tiny Capitola Cottage. The upholsterer delivered it on a day that Mike's son, my Godson, Peter Shaw, was visiting. He was the first to sit in it. When I sat in it, I could feel my father. It was almost like sitting on his lap. I snuggled beneath the afghan Mother crocheted years ago and considered putting my thumb in my mouth.

Full circle. I am comforted by my father's presence. In my home. In my heart. In my life. I needed the wing chair to make the house complete and can almost hear him giving me his supreme compliment, "You done good, Sis."

* This story was written in 1991 for Roxanne. Sarah Rankin illustrated it.

Things They've Said

Derek and Caitlin are Jane and Sam Love's children, my eldest grandchildren, born in the early 1980's, 13 months apart. A team of tigers from the beginning.

I think they must have been about 3 and 4 the weekend Sam and Jane dropped them off with me in San Mateo and went to Carmel to celebrate their wedding anniversary. I piled one on top of the other into the stroller and headed around the corner where we had fun racing around in the grade school play yard. In the afternoon, we walked with umbrellas in the rain. In the evening I lay with them on the floor to build blocks. They fingerpainted the bathtub tiles and soaked in bubbly warm water. They, indeed, were grand children!

They were not, however, fun at mealtime. They picked at their food. I fussed at them. They spilled their food. They smeared their food. By Sunday noon I walked away from the kitchen table, leaving them there with their quartered and trimmed peanut butter and jelly sandwiches. I no longer cared if they ate or pasted the bread on the wall. At the doorway, I turned and said, "Do what you like. When you're through, wipe your hands on this wet towel and come into the living room. I am going to lie down. I want you to play on the floor in the living room and not make a single sound. Be very quiet. I will be right there on the sofa."

They were quiet. Only an occasional muffled giggle. I heard their chairs scrape back from the table. I heard them sharing the towel, tugging it, dropping it onto the floor. They came stealthily into the living room, slowly poured the blocks out onto the carpet. The only sound was the careful click of blocks being stacked one on top of the other.

Then Derek whispered loudly to Caitlin, "I think Gran's had it."

In July of 1991 Mike and I, in love at 64, were married in the back garden of my home on Occidental Avenue in San Mateo. We had invited 60 of our closest relatives. I wore a creamy, flowery summer dress. As a final touch, I dropped my good pearls over my head and added pearl earrings.

Four generations arrived. All the women and girls wore flowery summer dresses. Sarah was three. Her blue flowered dress had a Peter Pan collar, her ankle socks had lace on the edges. She ran down the hallway toward me, her Mary Janes thumping, her bangs bobbing. I was braced to catch her in my arms when suddenly she stopped. Still six feet from me, her eyes big with excitement, her voice almost boomed. "Gran! We both wore our pearls!"

I wore them again last week when her mother and I attended the Los Altos High School wind ensemble concert, in which Sarah plays first flute.

⚜

One winter weekend a few years ago, granddaughter Jenny, then 10, and Katie, eight, had a sleep-over with me in Capitola. They had brushed their teeth, put on their nighties, and chosen their books. I was still downstairs when I heard Katie upstairs grunting and wheezing, working hard. "I can't open the bed!" she wailed. I went up to help and together we got her in bed. She propped herself among her pillows and I told her I was sorry I made the bed so tight. "Well," she summarized, "It looks good, but it doesn't work."

Important life lesson. It's ok to look good, but what's the use if it doesn't work.

⚜

In August of 2004, Matt and his eight-year-old daughter Jamie came over from Morgan Hill to pick the gravenstein apples from the neighbor's tree at the end of Garnet St. and we made applesauce together. Jamie forced the pulp through the strainer and

I collected the stems, seeds, and peelings in the sink. I was moaning about wasting it all and reminded Matt and Jamie about how we took buckets of apple leavings out to the sheep when we made applesauce on the farm in Oregon. As we continued to process the apples, Jamie was quiet for a while, then piped up, " Gran! I have an idea! We can mail the apple leavings to Mike and he can give them to the sheep!"

More recently, in December of 2004, I was prepared for our family's annual Grandmother's Crab Soup and Christmas Caroling Gathering. The soup was fragrant, the Christmas lights sparkled, the fire was laid, the candles lighted. Everyone arrived, happy to see each other. The party was swinging along well. I was pleased. The house was pretty. The effect just what I wanted. Then my son John came and whispered in my ear, "Are you sure you want your underwear drying on the shower rod?"

I was having dinner with John and Holly, Sarah, Jenny and Katie one evening in the spring of 2005. We talked about our totems, our favorite animal spirits. They knew mine is a giraffe. John mentioned a bear. Holly said hers is an owl. Sixteen-year-old Sarah hooted and said, "Mom! That is perfect for you!"

"Yes, Sarah?" Holly asked. "Why do you think so?"

"Because. You are always asking, 'Whooo is going to be there? Whooo is driving? Whooo are you going with?'"

Commencement Speeches

I have just finished reading Anne Lamott's <u>Plan B, Further Thoughts on Faith</u>. In the next to last chapter, she tells us the text of the speech she uses when asked to address college commencement graduates.

I like best, "From the wise old pinnacle of my years, I can tell you that what you're looking for is already inside you." And, "We can see Spirit made visible when people are kind to one another, especially when it's a really busy person, like you, taking care of a needy, annoying, neurotic person, like you."

She asks how do we feed and nourish our spirit and the spirit of others? And answers, "First find a path, and a little light to see by. Then push up our sleeves and start helping. Every single spiritual tradition says that you must take care of the poor. You don't have to go overseas. There are people in this country who are poor in spirit, worried, depressed, dancing as fast as they can; their kids are sick, or their retirement savings are gone. There is great loneliness among us, life-threatening loneliness. You do what you can, what good people have always done...you stand up for the underdog."

These comments are made by Annie Lamott to college graduates and their families. As I read them, I thought of another speech I heard in 2002. In Los Altos, my granddaughter Sarah Love was one of ten students to speak at their Eighth Grade Graduation. She titled her talk "We Are The Future" and started with a quote from Abraham Lincoln, "A child is a person who is going to carry on what you have started. He will assume control of your cities, states, and nations. He is going to move in and take over your churches, schools, universities, and corporations. The fate of humanity is in his hands."

Sarah continues, "I realize that we, the class of 2002, are the future. This is the biggest amount of responsibility and pressure in our lives. We cannot mess up. What will happen on the Earth for the next fifty years is in our hands. For example, we will affect whether society comes to have better values, or if it comes to have worse values. Our education prepares us to solve the problems of

Tell Me a Story

world hunger or we could start a nuclear war. For anything good to happen in this world, we must stand up for ourselves and for everything we believe in, because all that will happen depends on our generation. If someone makes a racist remark, don't stand there and let it happen. Tell them that racism is wrong. I for one am never going to judge a person based on their appearance or gender, and I truly hope that no one will discriminate against me because I am a girl."

Sarah closes with, "There are many things we can do to help our world. You could start a petition to save forestland from highways. I'll sign it. You could travel to Africa to help its people. I'll support you. We cannot stand and watch the Earth's peacefulness and beauty being destroyed. We will be here for a long time, and I, personally, would like it to be a good time. I don't want to ruin it. We only live once, so make the most of it! We are the future."

Annie Lamott finishes her speech to collegiate graduates, "You are capable of lives of great joy and meaning. It's what you are made of. And it's what you're here for. Take care of yourselves; take care of one another. And give thanks."

My mother used to say to us when we were children and she wanted us to get our chores done, "Commence now!" Annie Lamott and Sarah Love are showing us how.

Original artwork created for this book

Illustration by Katie Love, age 11

Photograph by Sarah Love, age 16

Illustration by Jamie Love, age 9